Skillsets For Sales Success, Built One Skill at a Time

THE SELLER'S FRAMEWORK
FROM SELLER TO SALES LEADER

*Move From Closing Deals to Leading People
& Driving Results*

TREVOR WEBER

© 2025 Trevor Weber. All rights reserved.

No part of this book may be reproduced, distributed, or transmitted in any form or by any means, including photocopying, recording, or other electronic or mechanical methods, without the prior written permission of the publisher, except in the case of brief quotations embodied in critical reviews and certain other noncommercial uses permitted by copyright law.

This book is a blend of fiction and nonfiction. The storyline and characters are fictional and used for illustrative purposes only. However, the principles, frameworks, and practical applications presented throughout are based on the author's professional experience, research, and real-world practice. Any resemblance to actual persons, living or dead, or actual events is purely coincidental.

Portions of this book were created with the assistance of AI-based writing tools under the direct authorship of the author.

For permission requests, contact the author.

ISBN: 9798271322280

Imprint: Independently published

Printed in the United States of America

First Edition

Dedicated to my wife, for supporting me through the successes and the failures, the long days and late nights–and for never giving up on me.

Acknowledgments

This book would not exist without the managers, mentors, and friends who have shaped my journey in sales and leadership over the past two decades.

Kevin & Gayle B.—for recognizing my potential in sales and giving me my very first sales role 20 years ago. That opportunity set everything else in motion.

JR—my first sales manager, who not only taught me the power of organization but also showed me what it means to be both a manager and a friend.

Noah C.—for showing me how to coach through numbers and metrics.

Jeff G.—an inspiring manager who stood by me through struggles and challenges, always reminding me to "just keep going."

Joey D.—for being both a strong manager and a loyal friend, and more importantly, a brother.

Tim B.—for teaching me to slow down, pay attention to the details, and recognize how much the little things matter.

Jason G.—for bringing humanity into management and modeling how empathy and leadership can work together.

Finally, to all those I've had the privilege of leading: thank you. You've helped me grow more than you know. You revealed my weaknesses, sharpened my strengths, and tested me in ways that refined my character and leadership. Each of you has shaped me as much as I have tried to support and guide you. For that, I am deeply grateful.

Contents

Series Preface   2

Preface   5

Introduction   9

CHAPTER ONE
Preparing for Leadership   15

CHAPTER TWO
Coaching in Action   25

CHAPTER THREE
Promoted   35

CHAPTER FOUR
Leading with HEART   43

CHAPTER FIVE
Identity Shift   55

CHAPTER SIX
Inspect What You Expect   67

CHAPTER SEVEN
Planning Leadership   79

CHAPTER EIGHT
Manager in the Middle   91

CHAPTER NINE
Coaching with Consistency — 104

CHAPTER TEN
Accountability and Performance Gaps — 115

CHAPTER ELEVEN
Cross-Department Collaboration — 125

CHAPTER TWELVE
Performance Plans — 135

CHAPTER THIRTEEN
Hiring Right — 147

CHAPTER FORTEEN
Leading Through Separation — 159

CHAPTER FIFTEEN
Turning Critics into Allies — 169

CHAPTER SIXTEEN
Sustaining Leadership — 179

Conclusion — 189

Reader Toolkit & Appendix — 195

Reference & Research Guide — 203

About the Author — 211

THANK YOU FOR YOUR PURCHASE!

I'm grateful you've taken the step to read *From Seller to Sales Leader*. It's the third book in a trilogy within *The Seller's Framework* sales series.

If you'd like to explore more books on sales & leadership, visit the Amazon link below or scan the QR code.

Thank you, again!

https://www.amazon.com/dp/B0G66M91Q3

Purchase more books in
The Seller's Framework series

Series Preface

The Seller's Framework series follows Jason's growth from brand-new account executive to seasoned seller and, ultimately, into sales leadership. Each book is designed to meet you where you are—whether you're just getting started, building momentum, or preparing to lead others.

Book 1 —
The Seller's Framework: The Fundamentals of Selling

This first book introduces the essential skills every seller needs to succeed early and build lasting confidence. Through Jason's journey and real-world frameworks, you'll learn how to uncover client needs, deliver value, and close deals with integrity. The goal is to help you lay a foundation strong enough to carry you through the challenges of a sales career, while also giving you a language and structure you can return to again and again.

Book 2 —
The Seller's Framework: Winning Complex Sales

In the second book of the series, the stakes rise as Jason enters the world of executive conversations and enterprise-level deals. This book equips you with tools to engage leaders, align with strategy, and navigate the complexity of larger buying groups. Whether you're preparing for your first executive call or seeking to sharpen your influence at the top levels, you'll find practical frameworks and examples to help you win buy-in, shorten sales cycles, and consistently deliver results in complex selling environments.

Book 3 —
The Seller's Framework: From Seller to Sales Leader

The final book in this trilogy shifts focus from individual selling to leading others. Jason's journey now mirrors the challenges of moving into management—coaching, developing teams, and driving performance while still carrying forward the principles that made him successful as a seller. This book gives you a roadmap for transitioning into leadership with confidence, showing you how to inspire people, manage results, and create a culture where sellers thrive. *Reader Sidenote: While not everyone will move into a leadership role, I encourage you to read book 3, as it provides insights into your manager's day, their focus, and what's important to them.*

Like Jason, you won't learn everything at once. Each book builds on the last. This series is designed to grow with you, giving you the tools to practice at each stage of your career. Most of the frameworks mentioned in these books will be expanded in future books of *The Seller's Framework* series **(for more information and estimated release dates, visit www.thesellersframework.com)**.

Read these books with the intent to apply. Sales mastery comes from discipline, reflection, and action. By the end of this series, you won't just know Jason's story, hopefully, you'll have written your own.

Preface

Stepping into leadership rarely feels like a smooth handoff. I learned that firsthand. Over the course of my career, I've reviewed and coached thousands of sales calls and meetings. One lesson became clear: no two sellers are exactly alike. What motivates one person can discourage another. What works brilliantly for one rep may fall flat for the next. Managing others isn't about cloning yourself or pushing the methods that worked for you, it's about knowing your people, elevating their strengths, and helping them find what works for them.

Of course, that perspective didn't come easily. I've stumbled through the realities most managers face. I've hired the right people and seen them lift an entire team's performance, and I've hired the wrong people whose attitude or behavior quietly eroded the culture. I've had to fire people and know immediately it was the right decision, and I've let others go only to realize later that I might have failed them with the wrong coaching or unclear expectations. I've coached too quickly, answering before listening long enough, and I've been on the receiving end of that kind of coaching myself.

I share this because I'm not perfect, and I don't pretend to be. But those experiences taught me a lasting truth: when you care for the people who drive the business, the business tends to take care of itself.

And here's another truth: there's no simple formula, framework, or book that will instantly make someone a great manager. Leadership is trial and error, mixed with patience and humility. It's listening more than speaking, learning from your missteps, and adjusting along the way. Frameworks and models help, but they don't do the work for you. My hope is that this book gives you a structure you can return to when things feel messy, not as a set of rigid rules, but as anchors for your leadership journey.

To keep the lessons practical, as with books 1 and 2, every chapter follows a repeatable structure:

- **Jason's Story** — real-world style scenarios that show the tension of leading, with both mistakes and breakthroughs.
- **Bad and Good Examples** — contrasting moments that highlight what works, what backfires, and why.
- **Frameworks** — easy-to-remember acronyms with intent, pitfalls, examples, and guardrails for clarity.
- **Research, Guardrails, and Quotes** — insights from proven leadership studies, cautions to avoid common traps, and encouragement from respected thinkers.
- **Reflection** — built around the rhythm of *Respond, Reflect, Repeat*.

Leadership isn't something you "arrive" at. It's something you practice. My hope is that Jason's story–his wins, his missteps, and his growth–helps you step into leadership with more clarity, confidence, and compassion.

With that, let's step back into Jason's world and see what leadership looks like in practice.

Introduction

"To lead people, walk beside them. When the best leaders' work is done, the people say, 'We did it ourselves.'"

Lao Tzu

Jason's journey so far has been anything but straightforward.

In Book 1, *The Fundamentals of Selling*, he stepped into enterprise sales for the first time. Guided by Maria, he learned the essentials of discovery, presenting, closing, and following up. Not as isolated skills, but as a connected system. He stumbled often, but each failure sharpened him.

In Book 2, *Winning Complex Sales*, Jason entered the executive arena. He discovered the difference between manager-level discovery and executive-level dialogue, learned how to multi-thread, and began speaking the language of ROI. He wrestled with CFOs, procurement, and the complexity of large, multi-stakeholder deals. Through it all, Maria continued to coach him into a true enterprise seller.

It's now been several months since Jason and his team closed the complex deal with Karen and Susan's company. Implementation is underway, and Jason has watched the solution he promised begin to take root inside their organization. His confidence has grown, not only from that win, but from several other large deals that followed. More importantly, his orchestration of internal resources and his ability to thread multiple client stakeholders together has stood out. Those skills caught Maria's eye, and leadership began to see Jason as more than a top performer. They saw influence.

That influence is why Jason has been tapped for a six-month leadership development track, the first step in transitioning from seller to leader.

This book isn't about closing your own deals anymore. It's about leading others to close theirs. Jason's world will shift from carrying his own number to carrying the weight of a team. From being measured on personal success to being accountable for the success of others. From "how well I sell" to "how well I coach, lead, and build."

How to Use This Book

The pages ahead aren't just a story, they're a roadmap. Each chapter follows Jason as he navigates the messy, real challenges of becoming a first-time manager: awkward performance conversations, balancing executive pressure with team morale, hiring and firing, dealing with difficult personalities, and shaping culture.

To get the most from this journey, I recommend you:

- Read one chapter per week.
- Reflect on the questions at the end of each chapter.
- Apply the concepts before moving forward.

Leadership isn't learned in a sprint. It's built in steady steps. By pacing yourself, you give time for each lesson to sink in and show up in your day-to-day life.

Aha! Moment

Just as sales success depends on consistency in discovery, presentations, and closing, leadership success depends on consistency in coaching, accountability, and culture.

Jason doesn't yet wear the title of manager. But Maria had pulled him aside and told him plainly: "If you want to lead, it starts now."

The months ahead will test Jason in ways selling never did. He'll be asked to mentor a rookie, shadow Maria in leadership settings, and begin acting like a leader while still carrying his own quota. Jason now feels the full tension of being caught between peer and manager, seller and leader.

His journey begins not with a promotion, but with preparation.

Introduction Reflection Questions

RESPOND: What motivated me to step into leadership, or to consider it?

REFLECT: Do I measure success only by my results, or by the growth of others?

REPEAT: What's one step I can take this week to apply leadership lessons, not just read them?

Preparing for Leadership

"He who cannot command himself will always be a servant."

Johann Wolfgang von Goethe

CHAPTER ONE

Jason had barely adjusted to the idea of being on a leadership track when the weight of his new role began to press down.

On paper, nothing had changed—he was still carrying his own number, chasing deals, and running demos. But now he was also mentoring Jordan, attending leadership meetings, and juggling training sessions that pulled him out of the field.

He thought he could handle it all. After all, he'd learned structure and discipline as a rep.

But leadership was different—it demanded presence, balance, and the ability to manage others while still delivering himself.

The cracks began to show.

Jason rushed from a prospect demo straight into a coaching session with Jordan.

Tired and distracted, he unloaded a long list of things Jordan needed to fix—speaking too fast, missing pain points, jumping to price, failing to set a follow-up. Jordan nodded quickly, but the conversation left him more overwhelmed than equipped.

Later that week, Jordan tried applying Jason's advice during a meeting. His delivery was rigid, rehearsed, and unnatural. The client disengaged halfway through, and the deal went cold.

Jason wasn't much better in his leadership meetings.

One afternoon, he slipped in late after Jordan had stopped him in the hallway with a question. He sat down distracted, glancing at his phone as two big deals ran through his head. When Maria asked about Jordan's progress, Jason mumbled a vague answer, eyes still on his screen.

He told himself he was just stretched thin—that this was temporary.

But deep down, he knew the truth: he was reacting, not leading.

He was multitasking through moments that required focus, wedging leadership into the cracks of his schedule.

Aha! Moment

Leadership begins with leading yourself. If you can't manage your time, presence, and priorities, you'll always be serving the chaos instead of commanding it.

Maria's Coaching

After the meeting, Maria caught Jason in the hallway. Her tone was calm but direct.

"Jason, I need to be honest. You're not showing up. You're trying to do everything, and it's showing. You rushed Jordan, you were late today, and in the meeting, you weren't really present. What's going on?"

Jason rubbed the back of his neck. "It's just…a lot. I've got deals I can't lose, Jordan pulling on me for coaching, leadership meetings, training. I feel like I'm failing somewhere no matter what I do."

Maria nodded. "That's because you're approaching leadership the same way you approached selling. When you were a rep, managing your own pipeline was enough. Now you're responsible for more than just results—you're responsible for people. And if you can't lead yourself first, you'll never be able to lead others."

Jason frowned. "So where do I even start?"

Maria leaned in slightly. "Anchor yourself in a framework that helps you focus on what matters most. Think of it as the word, leader—the fundamentals of leading well."

The LEADER Framework

Leadership doesn't come with a playbook. It's messy, demanding, and often learned through trial and error. That's why new managers need an anchor. The LEADER framework gives structure to the chaos, helping you manage yourself first, then extend that leadership outward to your team.

Lead Self

Self-leadership is the foundation of all leadership. It begins with managing your time, focus, and energy so you can show up intentionally. Great leaders don't drift through their calendars—they decide how they'll lead each moment before it begins. Many managers struggle because client pressure consumes their day, they say yes to everything, or they confuse busyness with productivity.

When you lead yourself first, you model discipline and purpose.

Examples
- Block prep time for coaching just as you would a client meeting.
- Do a quick "energy check" before each one-on-one to reset your focus.

- Protect time for strategic work rather than reacting to every ping.

Self-leadership isn't self-indulgence—it's stewardship. Manage your energy not to make life easier, but to serve your people better.

Engage Others

Leadership is relational. People follow those who make them feel seen, heard, and valued. Engagement transforms compliance into commitment—it's the bridge between authority and trust. Too often, managers rush through coaching sessions just to "check the box," listen to reply instead of listening to understand, or avoid uncomfortable conversations that would actually strengthen connection.

To build engagement

- Ask reflective questions that give reps ownership of their growth.
- Acknowledge emotions before jumping into problem-solving.
- Read nonverbal cues and surface unspoken concerns.

Engage deeply, but balance care with clarity. Empathy without accountability builds comfort, not progress.

Adapt with Flexibility

Every rep, deal, and situation is different. Leaders who adapt their approach build credibility and confidence. Flexibility doesn't mean lowering standards—it means meeting people where they are while keeping expectations firm. Some managers fail because they rely on one-size-fits-all coaching, resist necessary changes, or confuse adaptability with inconsistency.

Strong leaders adapt by

- Adjusting cadence when a rep needs more frequent check-ins.
- Switching between tactical and strategic coaching based on context.
- Experimenting with new tools when old systems slow progress.

Adapt methods, never principles. Be flexible in style, but firm in standards.

Develop People

True leadership multiplies capability, not dependency. Developing people means equipping them to think, decide, and grow beyond your daily guidance. Many managers hold their teams back by giving quick answers instead of helping reps find their own, focusing only on top or bottom performers, or mistaking training for real development.

To truly develop your people

- Ask reps to self-assess performance before giving feedback.
- Coach toward career goals, not just monthly metrics.
- Assign stretch projects that build confidence and capability.

Development builds independence, not reliance. Guide, don't rescue.

Empower Others

Empowerment is the transfer of trust. It's giving people ownership with clear boundaries so they grow through responsibility. Managers who micromanage, delegate without context, or withhold authority out of fear send the message that trust must be earned instead of given.

You empower others when you

- Let a rep lead part of a team meeting, then debrief afterward.
- Recognize initiative even when the outcome isn't perfect.
- Provide autonomy in decision-making while remaining available for guidance.

Empowerment without clarity creates chaos. Define direction first, then give freedom.

Reflect & Refine

Growth doesn't come from repetition—it comes from reflection. Reflection turns experience into improvement and ensures every week builds on the last. Leaders who rush from one task to the next without assessing progress, dismiss feedback because it's uncomfortable, or treat reflection as optional end up repeating mistakes instead of learning from them.

To refine consistently

- Journal one leadership insight at the end of each week.
- Ask for feedback from peers and reps alike.
- Review missed goals to identify root causes—not blame.

Reflection without change is nostalgia. Always turn lessons into next actions.

Note: The LEADER framework will be expanded in a future book within The Seller's Framework series. Visit www.thesellersframework.com for updates and release timelines.

> ### Research Spotlight: Leadership Anchors
> According to the *Center for Creative Leadership*, about 70 percent of leadership development comes from on-the-job experiences, not formal training. The leaders who grow fastest are those who intentionally reflect, adapt, and build self-awareness while developing others. Anchoring growth in simple frameworks like LEADER ensures lessons from experience actually stick and translate into performance.

The following week, Jason made deliberate changes. He blocked time for coaching Jordan and prepared thoughtful questions in advance. He also carved out quiet time in his calendar to focus on leadership tasks rather than letting client calls consume every hour. **(Lead Self)**

When Jordan recapped a recent client meeting, Jason resisted the urge to jump in.

"So," Jason asked, leaning forward, "How did you feel that call went?"

Jordan hesitated. "Not great. I think I rushed it."

"What made you feel rushed?" Jason prompted.

Jordan paused, thinking it through. "I was nervous about losing the deal. I wanted to prove I knew what I was doing."

Jason nodded. "I've been there. What could you try differently next time?" (**Engage Others**)

When a last-minute client issue threatened to overlap their session, Jason adapted instead of canceling. "Let's focus for twenty minutes. What's your biggest challenge right now?" (**Adapt with Flexibility**)

He encouraged Jordan to diagnose his own gaps first, then added his perspective. "You caught the signal but missed the meaning. Let's role-play how you could dig deeper next time." (**Develop People**)

By the end, Jordan smiled. "I actually feel more confident now."

"That's the goal," Jason said. "You've got this one." (**Empower Others**)

That evening, Jason opened his notebook and jotted down what worked, what didn't, and what he'd improve next time. He realized leadership wasn't a checklist, it was a rhythm of reflection, connection, and growth. (**Reflect & Refine**)

Chapter 1 Reflection Questions

RESPOND: What one adjustment will I make today to lead myself first, whether in time, focus, or presence?

_____
_____
_____
_____
_____

REFLECT: How has my tendency to react instead of lead impacted my team's trust or growth so far?

_____
_____
_____
_____
_____

REPEAT: What rhythm or practice (blocking prep time, journaling, pausing before coaching) will I commit to weekly, so self-leadership becomes a repeatable habit?

_____
_____
_____
_____
_____

Coaching in Action

"The art of coaching is unlocking a person's potential to maximize their own performance."

John Whitmore

CHAPTER TWO

With his calendar steadier and his head clearer, Jason shadowed one of Jordan's prospect calls to see if his coaching was landing.

At first, things looked fine: Jordan greeted the prospect warmly, asked a few openers, and tried to build rapport. But as the conversation unfolded, Jason's stomach tightened.

Jordan fell into the trap most new reps do—talking too much and too fast, rushing to unload product knowledge, and offering price before uncovering the real need.

Worst of all, when the prospect mentioned a challenge, Jordan missed it entirely and pushed for the close.

The meeting ended politely but without energy.

Jason, frustrated, jumped in as soon as the call disconnected.

"You talked too much, missed the pain point, and rushed the close. Next time, do this, this, and this."

Jordan nodded quickly, eyes fixed on his notebook, shoulders stiff. He didn't argue, but he didn't look encouraged either.

Later, on his next call, he tried parroting Jason's instructions word for word. It came out robotic. The prospect disengaged, and the deal slipped away.

Jason shook his head. "Why doesn't he just listen?" he muttered.

Aha! Moment

Coaching isn't about telling reps what to do; it's about helping them discover what they likely already know. People rarely own instructions, but they deeply own what they discover for themselves.

Maria's Coaching

Later that week, during Jason's one-on-one with Maria, she brought up Jordan.

"How are his calls going?" she asked.

Jason unloaded his frustration. "He talks too much, misses pain points, skips next steps...I spelled it all out for him, but he just doesn't get it."

Maria tilted her head. "And how did he respond when you gave all that feedback?"

Jason paused, replaying the moment. "Honestly? He shut down. He looked discouraged."

Maria leaned forward. "Jason, let me ask you this: when you were in his shoes, what kind of coaching helped you most?"

Jason thought back to his early days. "When you asked me questions. It forced me to think, not just repeat what you told me."

"Exactly," Maria said. "Coaching is like discovery in sales. You don't win by pitching—you win by asking. Seek understanding first. Help them clarify what happened, give them space to reflect, and then expand their perspective. If you jump straight to telling, you miss the chance to develop."

The COACH Framework

Coaching isn't about having all the answers—it's about helping others discover their own. Great leaders know that the best insights come from within the person being coached, not from the person giving direction.

The COACH framework gives leaders a repeatable structure to guide development conversations that unlock growth, ownership, and lasting change.

Clarify the Situation

Every meaningful coaching conversation starts with clarity. Before giving direction, take time to understand what actually happened and what the rep was aiming for.

Many leaders jump in with advice before knowing the full picture, assume they already understand the goal, or focus only on what went wrong instead of what the rep was trying to accomplish. By slowing down to clarify both the facts and intentions, you prevent assumptions, reduce defensiveness, and create space for productive dialogue.

You could start by asking

- "Walk me through what you were hoping to achieve in that call."
- "What did success look like for you going in?"
- "If everything had gone perfectly, what would the outcome have been?"

Clarify both the event and the desired outcome—not just one or the other. This keeps the focus on learning, not blame, and ensures both of you are solving the same problem.

Offer Space & Observe

Coaching isn't about controlling the pace of the conversation—it's about creating space for reflection. Silence gives people room to process, reflect, and reveal what's really going on.

Often, leaders talk over reps, fill every silence, or rush to their next question before truly listening. By observing tone, pauses, and body language, you can uncover unspoken challenges and deeper motivations that words alone might miss.

You might

- Pause intentionally for 5–10 seconds after asking a question.
- Notice tone shifts or hesitation when specific topics arise.
- Reflect what you observe: "I noticed your energy dropped when you mentioned that—what's behind it?"

Resist the urge to fill silence or fix discomfort too quickly. The best insights surface when you let the rep work through their own thoughts before stepping in.

Ask Powerful Questions

The quality of a leader's questions determines the quality of their team's thinking. Powerful questions challenge assumptions and help reps recognize blind spots, strengthen self-awareness, and take ownership of their improvement.

Leaders sometimes fall into habits that limit reflection—asking yes-or-no questions, steering conversations toward their preferred answer, or firing off too many questions at once. Instead, ask questions that create pause and curiosity, guiding the rep to uncover their own insights.

Try questions such as

- "Where did momentum shift in that meeting?"
- "If you could redo one part, what would you try differently?"
- "What did you notice about the client's reaction when you explained pricing?"

Your goal isn't to sound smart—it's to spark thought. Ask fewer, better questions that guide the rep toward insight. Remember, if you want a better answer, ask a better question.

Confirm Understanding

Once insights begin to emerge, pause to ensure alignment. Confirming understanding strengthens clarity on what was said, what was meant, and what will change moving forward.

Leaders sometimes assume alignment without verifying it, dominate the recap with their own interpretation, or move on before the rep feels heard. Taking a moment to confirm understanding builds trust and reinforces that coaching is a partnership built on mutual respect, not a one-way critique.

You might say

- "So, you felt momentum dipped after discovery. That matches what I noticed."

- "Let's make sure we agree on the main challenge here."
- "It sounds like you're saying the client's hesitation caught you off guard. Is that right?"

Keep the recap collaborative and mutual. Confirmation creates psychological safety—a shared understanding that drives confidence and consistency.

Help Expand Perspective

This is where you add value as a leader—by offering perspective the rep may not see yet. Expand their awareness by highlighting a blind spot or introducing a next step that stretches their thinking.

Be careful to avoid overwhelming reps with too many takeaways, fix the issue for them, or share advice with no connection to what was discussed. True coaching balances insight with accountability, giving guidance without removing ownership.

You could say

- "One area you didn't mention was the budget step—that's worth focusing on."
- "Here's one approach that works when momentum dips."
- "You're strong at rapport, but your follow-up plan could use tightening. How could you address that?"

Less is more. Focus on one actionable step that moves the conversation forward. Accountability is a key part of coaching—but that topic deserves its own framework later.

Note: The COACH framework will be expanded further in a future mini-book of The Seller's Framework series. For updates and release dates, visit www.thesellersframework.com.

> ### Research Spotlight:
> ### The Measurable Impact of Sales Coaching
>
> *CSO insights* found that organizations achieve win rates at 19% higher and quota attainment 27.9% higher when sales professionals receive structured coaching
>
> Salespeople receiving more than nine hours of weekly coaching outperformed peers by 7% on average (*Sales Management Association*, 2018).
>
> Together, these studies underline the point: coaching isn't a soft skill, it's a sales performance multiplier. Structured frameworks like COACH keep managers from winging it and ensure reps consistently grow in ways that directly improve revenue outcomes.

On Jordan's next call, Jason took a different approach. Instead of critiquing, he leaned back and asked:

"What did you feel went well?" (**Clarify**)

Jordan paused, then replied, "I think I did a better job of setting the agenda up front."

Jason nodded. "Where did you feel momentum dipped?" (**Ask**)

Jordan thought for a moment. "After discovery. I didn't know how to transition into budget without sounding pushy."

Jason let the silence sit before asking, "What could you have done differently to keep momentum?" (**Offer Space & Ask**)

Jordan frowned, then slowly answered, "I could have asked about next steps tied to their goals before bringing up budget."

Jason smiled. "Exactly—that's the adjustment. And one more thing I noticed: you skipped the budget piece entirely. That's something to strengthen." **(Help Expand)**

Jordan walked away from their meeting energized and confident, like he'd uncovered his own path forward. Jason felt it too—the shift from giving answers to guiding discovery.

In the weeks ahead, the change spread. Jordan steadied, Maya leaned in, and Jason's leadership started to take shape. Maria saw it first—and soon, leadership did too.

Chapter 2 Reflection Questions

RESPOND: What part(s) of the COACH framework do I need to improve in my feedback conversations?

_____
_____
_____
_____
_____

REFLECT: Do you default to giving answers, or do you draw out awareness with questions?

_____
_____
_____
_____
_____

REPEAT: What's one coaching conversation you can revisit this week with a COACH approach?

_____
_____
_____
_____
_____

Promoted

"The challenge of leadership is to be strong, but not rude; to be kind, but not weak; to be bold, but not a bully; to be thoughtful, but not lazy; to be humble, but not timid; to be proud, but not arrogant; to have humor, but without folly."

Jim Rohn

The news came on a Tuesday morning.

Maria called Jason into her office, her expression unreadable.

"I've been asked to step into a broader role," she said. "And leadership has decided you're ready to take my place as manager."

For a moment, Jason just stared. The words felt heavy and unreal. *Promoted. Manager.* Recognition for the long hours, the wins, the grind that had defined his career. Pride swelled in his chest as he left Maria's office—the kind that comes when years of effort finally pay off.

At first, it felt like pure validation.

Maya, steady and dependable, congratulated him warmly.

Jordan's enthusiasm was contagious, his energy full of belief.

Samantha, the grinder of the group, offered a cautious smile. "Just don't forget what it's like in the trenches," she said.

And Alex, sharp and outspoken as ever, muttered, "What's Jason possibly going to coach me on?"

Jason laughed it off, but the words stayed with him.

In the days that followed, the excitement gave way to unease.

He tried to ease the transition by still acting like "one of the team." He joined in the banter, joked about leadership decisions he barely understood, and hinted that he missed being "just a rep."

But the more he tried to stay close, the less credible he felt.

The shift he'd earned began slipping away. The respect he once carried as a top performer now seemed uncertain.

Jason found himself caught between two worlds—the rep he'd been and the leader he was expected to become.

Aha! Moment

*Promotion isn't the finish line of selling;
it's the starting line of leadership.*

Maria's Coaching

Maria noticed the tension almost immediately.

She invited Jason into her office and waited until the door closed before speaking.

"Jason," she began, "this isn't about proving you earned the promotion. It's about growing into it. You can't keep leading like a rep—competing, blending in, and trying to be everyone's friend. They need a leader who listens, decides, and guides."

Jason nodded slowly. "It's hard, Maria. They were my peers. Now I'm their manager. I don't want to come across as arrogant or disconnected."

Maria leaned forward. "That balance is what separates good managers from great ones. Leadership starts with how you think, not just what you do. The habits that made you a great rep won't carry you here—they'll actually hold you back. You need to learn to think differently."

Jason frowned. "Think differently? How?"

"Think like a leader," Maria said. "A rep asks, 'How do I win?' A leader asks, 'How do we win?' The shift starts in your mindset long before it shows in your behavior."

Teaching

The transition from top performer to new leader is one of the hardest shifts in any career. Many new managers stumble because they carry a seller's mindset into leadership—focused on personal performance, speed, and recognition. Those same instincts that once made them stand out can now work against them.

A seller focuses on execution—controlling what they can, proving their capability, and earning results.

A leader must focus on enablement—guiding others, building systems, and developing people who perform even when they're not in the room.

The mental rewiring required isn't instant. It takes awareness, humility, and deliberate practice.

Research shows that only a small percentage of high performers naturally succeed as managers. The difference isn't talent—it's mindset. The most successful new leaders intentionally slow down, shift focus from "I" to "we," and measure success by how others grow.

Leaders who make this shift stop chasing personal wins and start building collective ones. They redefine achievement not as personal output, but as the development, engagement, and success of the people around them.

> ## Research Spotlight:
> ## Why Top Performers Struggle, and How They Succeed
>
> *Gallup* finds only 1 in 10 people naturally possess high managerial talent; companies that select and develop managers based on talent see markedly higher engagement.
>
> Yet, the same study found that managers who receive intentional coaching and development improve team engagement by up to 59%. The key isn't natural ability; it's mindset and support. Leadership success comes to those who are willing to grow into the role.

The next morning, Jason came in early, replaying Maria's words.

If leadership started with thinking differently, then his actions had to reflect that.

When the team gathered for pipeline review, the energy felt off.

Alex leaned back, arms crossed. "Another change in lead distribution," he said. "Leadership always makes sure the best ones go somewhere else." He glanced at Jason, expecting him to agree.

Jason took a breath. "I get it, Alex. It's frustrating when things feel uneven," he said, steady but calm. "But let's focus on what's still in our control. How do we make the most of the leads we do have?"

Jordan nodded thoughtfully. "Maybe we tighten our prep before the first call," he offered.

Maya added, "And share quick wins more often—maybe in our chat?"

The conversation shifted. Instead of complaints, ideas filled the room. Jason didn't dominate the discussion or try to prove himself—he guided it. His tone carried conviction without force, humility without hesitation.

When the meeting wrapped, Jason caught Maria watching from the doorway. She smiled, gave a small nod, and left without a word.

Jason exhaled slowly. The title hadn't made him a leader—the mindset had.

Over the next few days, Jason began to see leadership differently. It wasn't about being the best anymore; it was about bringing out the best in others. That realization would be tested soon, as the realities of his new role—expectations, metrics, and managing performance—began to take shape.

Chapter 3 Reflection Questions

RESPOND: What will you do in your very next interaction to show up as a leader, not just a peer?

_____

_____

_____

_____

_____

REFLECT: Where are you still relying on your identity as a rep instead of expanding into leadership?

_____

_____

_____

_____

_____

REPEAT: What practice will you establish (framing meetings, clarifying expectations, reinforcing growth) to consistently lead from your new identity?

_____

_____

_____

_____

_____

Leading with HEART

"Vulnerability is not a weakness. That myth is profoundly dangerous."

Brené Brown

Jason walked into his team meeting with a plan.

He wanted to project control—steady, confident, composed.

The agenda was simple: pipeline updates, coaching conversations, and alignment on next steps.

But it didn't go that way.

Halfway through the meeting, Maya spoke up, her tone calm but edged with frustration.

"Jason, I have to be honest, some of this coaching feels a little out of touch with what's happening in the field," she said. "It sounds great in theory, but it doesn't always land with clients."

Jason's eyes flicked up from his notes. "What part doesn't land?" he asked, his tone sharper than he intended.

Maya hesitated, glancing toward Jordan. "It's not one part exactly…it's more the tone. Clients are pushing back harder lately, and some of these responses come across too scripted."

Jason felt the flush rise in his neck. "Scripted?" he repeated. "I've been in those same conversations, Maya. The process works if you follow it."

Her brow furrowed. "I'm not saying the process is wrong."

"Then what are you saying?" Jason cut in, voice tight.

The room went still. Samantha shifted in her seat. Jordan's pen froze mid-scribble. Alex leaned back, smirking as if to say, *here we go.*

Maya's tone softened. "I'm just saying not every client fits the playbook. Sometimes we have to adjust."

Jason let out a breath that sounded more like a sigh. "Look, the playbook exists for a reason. We start changing it every time someone gets pushback, we lose consistency."

Silence pressed in. No one met his eyes.

Jason forced a quick smile, pretending to move on. "Alright, let's keep going—pipeline updates."

But the energy had shifted. The rest of the meeting dragged, his words falling flat.

By the time it ended, the room felt quieter, like the oxygen had been drained out.

Later that night, replaying the conversation, Jason realized it wasn't *what* he said. It was *how* he said it.

The defensiveness, the sharpness—it shut down Maya and everything he wanted the team to become.

Aha! Moment

Leadership isn't only about strategy, metrics, or execution. It's about emotion. The way leaders show up-tone, posture, and presence-shapes how the team performs and trusts.

Maria's Coaching

Maria heard about the tension before Jason had even processed it.

She motioned for him to close the door.

"Jason, I heard your meeting was rough. What emotional state were you in when Maya pushed back?"

He rubbed his neck. "Frustrated. It felt like she was questioning me in front of everyone."

"And how did you respond?"

"I snapped. Defensive."

Maria nodded. "And what happened to the room?"

"They shut down," Jason admitted. "I lost them."

Maria leaned forward. "Exactly. Leadership isn't just about being right—it's about managing how you show up. Your reaction sets the emotional temperature for the team. Vulnerability breeds vulnerability; defensiveness breeds silence."

She paused. "If you want to lead well, Jason, you have to lead with **HEART**."

The HEART Framework

Command-and-control leadership can drive compliance, but not commitment. Compliance may be necessary in moments of urgency or risk, but when it lacks empathy and heart, it breeds fear and disengagement.

The HEART framework anchors emotional intelligence in five behaviors every leader can practice, balancing accountability with empathy and authority with authenticity.

Humility (Self-Awareness)

Leadership starts with knowing yourself—your triggers, blind spots, and limitations. Humility isn't weakness; it's awareness. The willingness to admit mistakes, ask for input, and put others before yourself earns far more credibility than flawless execution ever will.

Leaders lose trust when they act as though they always have the answers, ignore how their tone or body language affects others, or confuse confidence with superiority. Practicing humility creates space for honest feedback and genuine connection.

You can demonstrate humility by

- Admitting when you've missed something and inviting team input.
- Doing a quick "emotional check-in" before a high-stakes meeting.
- Acknowledging stress rather than pretending it isn't there.

Humility doesn't mean self-doubt or self-deprecation. Lead with confidence and curiosity—own the role while staying teachable.

Emotional Regulation (Self-Management)

Under pressure, emotional steadiness communicates safety. Emotional regulation is the ability to pause, reflect, and choose your response rather than react impulsively.

Many leaders slip when frustration leaks out as sarcasm, stress dictates tone, or they overcorrect by suppressing emotion entirely. Regulation isn't about denial—it's about direction. Before responding, pause and ask yourself, "Is my reaction proportionate to the cause?"

You might

- Take a breath before responding to criticism.
- Ask a colleague for perspective before replying to a difficult email.
- Name the emotion ("I'm frustrated right now") to reduce its grip.

Regulation means directing emotions, not denying them. Check your own temperature first, then decide if your response will build or break trust.

Attunement (Social Awareness)

Great leaders read the room. Attunement is the ability to sense what's unsaid—tone, posture, hesitation—and address it directly. It transforms meetings from mechanical updates into meaningful conversations where people feel understood.

Leaders can mistakenly miss cues by ignoring subtle signs of disengagement, assuming silence means agreement, or plowing through agendas despite visible tension. Attunement invites honesty and restores focus.

In practice, you can

- Say, "I sense some hesitation. What's on your mind?"
- Spot when silence signals confusion rather than consensus.
- Adjust pace or tone when team energy dips.

Attunement isn't mind-reading. Observe, ask, and verify before you interpret.

Relationship Building (Empathy in Action)

Leadership is influence, not control. Relationship building turns compliance into commitment by connecting personally while holding standards professionally. When people feel seen and supported, they'll go further and stay longer.

Leaders fall short when they treat reps as quota carriers, only engage when performance drops, or delegate without context or care. Building authentic relationships means weaving empathy into everyday interactions, not waiting for problems to appear.

You can strengthen relationships by

- Connecting coaching conversations to each rep's career goals.
- Checking in on personal milestones or challenges.
- Celebrating effort, not just outcomes.

Relationship isn't friendship. Empathy must walk hand-in-hand with accountability—care without standards breeds complacency.

Trust (Credibility & Consistency)

Trust is leadership's currency—earned through fairness, follow-through, and transparency. Consistency under pressure builds loyalty that titles never can.

Leaders erode trust when they make promises they don't deliver on, show favoritism, or avoid hard calls to stay liked. Trust grows when words and actions align, even in difficult moments.

To build trust

- Follow through on even small commitments.
- Apply feedback and performance standards evenly across the team.
- Be transparent about decisions that impact others.

Trust doesn't mean avoiding hard truths. Fair accountability builds trust when it's delivered with clarity and respect.

Note: The HEART framework will be expanded in a future mini book within The Seller's Framework series. For updates and release timelines, visit www.thesellersframework.com.

> ### Research Spotlight: Why HEART Matters for Leaders
>
> Emotional intelligence is one of the strongest predictors of leadership success.
>
> According to research published in *The Journal of Applied Psychology,* empathetic leaders are more likely to create a culture of psychological safety.
>
> HEART isn't "soft." It's strategic—anchoring leadership behaviors in awareness, empathy, and trust so every interaction builds credibility and connection.

The following week, Jason entered the team meeting differently —calmer, centered.

He opened with honesty. "Last time, I was defensive. That's on me. I want this to be a space where feedback flows both ways, and I shut that down. You deserved better." (**Humility**)

The team glanced at each other; the tension eased.

Midway through, Samantha admitted, "I'm struggling to build a pipeline. I feel like I'm spinning."

Jason felt the old urge to fix it. He caught himself and drew a slow breath.

"What's making it toughest right now?" (**Emotional Regulation**)

Samantha blinked, surprised by the gentleness. "Honestly? I think I'm overcomplicating my prospecting."

Before Jason could respond, Maya shifted in her seat. "I have an idea for her, but I didn't want to interrupt."

Jason turned toward her. "Please, go ahead." (**Attunement**)

As Maya shared, Jason nodded. "That's a strong point, Maya. It's clear you've been refining your approach. How's that aligning with your development goal of leading more client strategy calls?" (**Relationship Building**)

The discussion flowed. Jordan added notes to the whiteboard; Alex even tossed out a few constructive suggestions.

Before closing, Jason revisited a commitment from last week—the competitive battle-card resource he'd promised.

"It's finished and uploaded this morning," he said. "Thanks for holding me to it." (**Trust**)

When the meeting ended, Maya lingered behind. "Hey, thanks for how you handled that," she said quietly. "That felt…different."

Jason smiled. "Good. Different is the goal."

He walked out realizing that leadership wasn't about defending his authority—it was about directing his energy.

Vulnerability had opened the door, and the team was finally walking through it with him.

Chapter 4 Reflection Questions

RESPOND: What situations or conversations tend to trigger strong emotions in you as a leader?

_____
_____
_____
_____
_____

REFLECT: When has your emotional reaction shaped your team's response, for better or worse?

_____
_____
_____
_____
_____

REPEAT: What daily HEART habit can you practice until it becomes part of your natural leadership style?

_____
_____
_____
_____
_____

Identity Shift

"Before you are a leader, success is all about growing yourself. When you become a leader, success is all about growing others."

– **Jack Welch**

CHAPTER FIVE

In the weeks following his promotion, Jason felt the pressure build.

Every meeting, every call, every result now reflected on him. He told himself he needed to prove he deserved the role.

That pressure showed up in subtle ways.

In team meetings, he spoke first instead of drawing others out. When Jordan asked for feedback on a proposal, Jason offered to "review it quickly"—then found himself rewriting half of it.

The line between supporting and doing blurred faster than he expected.

The real test came with Samantha, one of the more struggling reps.

Jason agreed to shadow a call with her, intending to support and debrief afterward. At first, the conversation moved steadily, but when a manager-level prospect raised a tough objection, Samantha froze. Silence stretched.

Jason's instincts kicked in. He jumped in, reframed the objection, handled the pushback, and steered the conversation to a next step.

On paper, it was a win. The deal advanced.

But Samantha's face told a different story—embarrassed, frustrated, and shut down. She hadn't grown; she'd been sidelined.

Later that afternoon, Alex leaned over Jason's desk with a grin that didn't quite hide the jab. "Heard you had to bail Samantha out. Guess some lessons are better taught by doing them yourself, huh?"

Jason managed a thin smile. "Something like that."

But the victory already felt hollow. Deep down, he knew: the team wasn't seeing a leader—they were seeing a rep who couldn't stop jumping back in.

Aha! Moment

Without an identity anchor, leaders drift back into old habits, confusing their teams and eroding trust. To lead well, you must intentionally ground your identity in developing others, not doing it all yourself.

Maria's Coaching

After Alex's comment, Jason didn't brush it off—this time, he went straight to Maria.

She looked up from her laptop as he walked in. "You look like someone carrying more than a pipeline review," she said.

Jason sighed. "I stepped in on Samantha's call. She froze, and I panicked. I didn't want to lose the deal, so I just...took over."

Maria nodded slowly. "And what did she take away from that?"

Jason thought for a moment. "That I don't trust her? Or maybe that she can't handle tough calls."

"Good awareness," Maria said. "Why do you think you jumped in so quickly?"

Jason hesitated. "Honestly? Fear. If the deal slipped, it would look bad on both of us. I figured stepping in was safer."

Maria tilted her head. "So it wasn't about proving yourself—it was about avoiding loss."

Jason nodded quietly. "Yeah. I didn't even think, I just reacted."

"That's the trap," Maria said. "You rescued the deal, but you robbed her of learning. Leadership isn't about saving moments; it's about developing people. Your job isn't to carry them—it's to enable them."

She paused, letting the word hang.

"Let's use a framework that will help you decide when to step in, when to guide, and when to step back—one that anchors your identity as a leader."

The ENABLE Framework

Stepping into leadership means shifting from doing to developing. New managers often drift back into selling because it feels faster, safer, and familiar. But every time you rescue a deal, rewrite a proposal, or take control of a client call, you weaken your credibility as a leader and your rep's confidence. That's why leaders need a guide when pressure mounts.

The ENABLE framework provides that anchor—reminding you that your role isn't to perform, but to help others perform.

Empower, Don't Rescue

Equip reps to handle challenges on their own so they build skill and confidence. Empowerment develops long-term strength; rescuing creates dependency.

When pressure rises, many leaders step in too quickly—jumping in to "fix" a meeting the moment a rep struggles, taking over projects because it feels faster, or over-coaching in real time until reps become spectators. These habits solve short-term problems but erode long-term capability.

You can build empowerment by

- Asking, "What options do you see here?" instead of giving the answer.
- Letting a rep finish a tough call, then debriefing afterward.
- Sharing frameworks that strengthen decision-making rather than dictating steps.

Step in only when business risk is high or a key account is truly at stake. When you intervene, make it teachable, not habitual.

Navigate Obstacles Together

Leaders walk beside their people, not ahead of them. Guiding means helping reps find their own path through challenges while shaping their thinking along the way.

Often, managers solve problems privately and then present finished solutions, shield reps from difficulty to protect them, or avoid collaboration because it slows progress. But walking through obstacles together strengthens ownership and thinking.

Consider

- Co-creating an objection-handling plan.
- Brainstorming ways to revive a stalled account.
- Discussing next steps together before finalizing decisions.

Begin with their ideas first. Your goal is to refine, not replace, their thinking.

Align Expectations & Roles

Clarity creates accountability. When expectations are aligned, reps know what's theirs to own and what support they can count on.

Confusion builds when ownership is left vague, when managers take control "to ensure quality," or when roles blur between who leads and who supports. Clear alignment keeps accountability in the right hands and performance on track.

You can set alignment by

- Clarifying who owns data gathering, pricing, and client delivery before building a proposal.
- Defining clear follow-up steps after a call so ownership is visible.
- Establishing timelines and check-ins before projects begin.

Define ownership, confirm understanding, and revisit agreements as projects evolve. Accountability should stay with the rep, not the manager.

Build Confidence

Confidence fuels capability. It grows when people are challenged, trusted, and recognized—not when they're constantly corrected or shielded from mistakes.

Leaders unintentionally weaken confidence when they only offer critique, protect reps from stretch opportunities, or fix problems before their team can try again. Confidence builds through autonomy and reinforcement, especially when performance wavers.

To build it

- Celebrate skill improvement, not just quota wins.
- Give reps space to present or lead internal sessions.
- Frame mistakes as feedback loops, not failures.

Encourage without lowering standards. Confidence grows strongest under challenge when it's supported with trust and feedback.

Lead by Example

Modeling inspires trust. True leadership balances showing the way with creating space for others to follow.

Managers often model excellence once, then take control again, talk about development without demonstrating growth themselves, or expect accountability they don't model personally. Leading by example means living the standards you expect and demonstrating the behaviors you want repeated.

You could

- Demonstrate an effective discovery call, then hand the next one to the rep.
- Share your own learning mistakes to normalize growth.
- Embody the same accountability you expect from your team.

Demonstrate first, delegate second. Use modeling as a launchpad—not a permanent crutch.

Establish Consistency & Feedback Loops

Consistency creates trust and rhythm. Regular feedback, steady routines, and predictable coaching make leadership dependable and reduce uncertainty.

Inconsistency undermines confidence. Leaders who cancel one-on-ones when deals heat up, only give feedback during crises, or constantly change direction leave reps unsure where they stand. Consistent presence turns leadership into stability, even during volatility.

You can reinforce consistency by

- Holding weekly one-on-ones no matter how busy the quarter gets.
- Ending projects with debriefs focused on lessons learned.
- Keeping notes to track growth across months, not just weeks.

Let reps struggle, even fail, as long as learning follows. Consistency doesn't mean saving them every time—it means being there every time to guide reflection.

Note: The ENABLE framework will be expanded in a future mini book within The Seller's Framework series. For updates and release timelines, visit www.thesellersframework.com.

Research Spotlight: Why ENABLE Matters

Linda Hill's *Becoming a Manager* (Harvard Press) showed that first-time leaders who resist rescuing behaviors build stronger, more confident teams within their first year.

> When leaders enable rather than rescue, performance and engagement rise together. Empowerment doesn't slow success—it multiplies it.

The next week, Jason decided to change his approach.

When Jordan brought him a draft proposal, Jason fought the urge to take the keyboard. "Walk me through your thinking," he said.

Instead of rewriting it, he asked questions that helped Jordan refine his own work. Jordan left owning the plan—and believing in it. (**Empower**)

When Samantha prepared for another client call, Jason sat beside her. "What approaches could you use if they push back on price?" he asked.

Together they mapped out strategies, but Samantha led the plan. (**Navigate**)

At the next huddle, Jason clarified roles. "You own your accounts. I'll coach and support, but results are yours."

He kept repeating that message until no one wondered who owned what. (**Align**)

He started highlighting progress in team meetings. When Maya shared a win, Jason said, "The way you slowed down and probed deeper—that's what built trust."

Recognition became fuel for confidence. (**Build**)

Occasionally he still modeled, but differently. During coaching, he demonstrated one discovery question, then smiled. "Your turn." **(Lead)**

And he kept a rhythm. One-on-ones stayed locked on the calendar.

Every Friday ended with reflection: what worked, what didn't, what to change next week. **(Establish)**

Samantha felt supported without being overshadowed. Jordan gained independence.

Even Alex, though still skeptical, began leaning in. The team wasn't watching Jason "prove himself" anymore—they were watching him enable them.

As Jason steadied his new leadership footing, a bigger test loomed ahead—his first full pipeline and forecast review.

Chapter 5 Reflection Questions

RESPOND: When was the last time you stepped in instead of enabling your team to own the outcome?

_____
_____
_____
_____
_____

REFLECT: Where are you still clinging to the doer identity instead of the developer's mindset?

_____
_____
_____
_____
_____

REPEAT: What ENABLE behavior can you focus on this week until it becomes second nature?

_____
_____
_____
_____
_____

Inspect What You Expect

"Don't expect what you don't inspect."

W. Edwards Deming

CHAPTER SIX

The Seller's Framework – From Seller to Sale

It had been a few months since Jason's promotion into the leadership track.

The team was finding rhythm, but his first formal pipeline and forecast review with Maria and the VP felt like walking into a test he hadn't fully studied for.

He knew the numbers mattered—they always had. But this time, it wasn't about his own pipeline. It was about his team's, and he'd relied too heavily on what his reps had told him in one-on-ones. Surely that would be enough.

The VP wasted no time. "Jason, let's start with Samantha," he began. "You've got her down for $150K this quarter. Which deals make that up?"

Jason hesitated, flipping through his notes. "Uh...she's working Acme and Horizon. Both are moving forward."

The VP raised an eyebrow. "Moving forward, how? What stage are they in, and how do you know they'll close this quarter?"

Jason's throat tightened. "That's what Samantha told me...they're committed."

The VP pressed. "Committed based on what? Do we have budget confirmed? Decision-maker alignment?"

Jason glanced at Maria, who stayed quiet, letting the silence speak.

"I don't have those details," he finally admitted.

The VP shifted to Jordan. "Okay, his forecast dropped by nearly half since last week. Why?"

Jason shuffled his papers again. "He told me one of the deals pushed out."

"Which one? Why?"

Jason paused. "I'd have to check."

The VP leaned back, expression flat. "Jason, you can't roll up a forecast just on what your reps say. I need you to know their deals well enough to defend why this number is real."

Jason nodded, his face warm. He wasn't dodging—he simply didn't know. And that, he realized, was worse.

Aha! Moment

Forecasts aren't about hope, they're about proof. Leaders can't simply roll up what their reps say. They must inspect the details, challenge assumptions, and build forecasts on evidence, not optimism.

Maria's Coaching

After the meeting, Maria caught Jason in the hallway. Her tone was calm, but her questions cut deep.

"Jason, when you called those deals a commit, what proof did you have?"

Jason hesitated. "I... trusted what the reps told me."

Maria nodded. "And if the deal slips, what happens to your credibility with leadership?"

Jason shifted uncomfortably. "I guess it takes a hit."

"Exactly," Maria said. "Forecasting isn't about repeating what you hear—it's about knowing what you can prove. How will you start inspecting what you expect from your team?"

Jason didn't have an answer yet, but he knew she was right.

He needed discipline, not just trust.

The INSPECT Framework

Pipeline and forecast reviews aren't about guesswork—they're about disciplined inspection. The INSPECT framework helps leaders move from hopeful forecasts to evidence-based confidence, separating strong deals from wishful ones and coaching their teams to do the same.

Inputs

Strong forecasts start with clean inputs. If the data foundation is weak, every forecast built on it is shaky. Clean inputs give leaders visibility, predictability, and credibility when reporting upward.

Many managers allow placeholders to linger, roll up inaccurate data, or treat CRM entry as administrative work rather than a leadership tool. The moment you stop inspecting inputs, accuracy begins to erode—and with it, your ability to lead with confidence.

You can improve data quality by

- Running a weekly hygiene check for deal amounts, close dates, and next steps.

- Requiring each opportunity to have an active contact and logged activity.
- Auditing stage accuracy before each forecast submission.

Don't turn inspection into policing. The goal is to coach reps on why clean data matters—inspection should drive better habits, not fear or punishment.

Numbers

Numbers tell the story of coverage, conversion, and capacity. Leaders must know if the math supports the message. A sound forecast is both quantitative and qualitative—grounded in ratios, not wishes.

The danger comes when managers rely on gut feel, ignore stage conversion rates, or overestimate confidence without verifying the math beneath it. Forecasting isn't about guessing—it's about measuring what's true.

You can bring discipline to your numbers by

- Calculating 3–4× coverage against quota and monitoring stage drop-offs.
- Comparing week-over-week changes to spot unusual swings.
- Flagging underweighted pipelines early to coach activity gaps.

Numbers guide the story but don't replace it. They provide the logic, not the full truth—context and judgment must always accompany the data.

Signals

Signals separate real opportunities from wishful thinking. Leaders must coach reps to identify concrete buying indicators—pain, urgency, budget, and decision process—before a deal earns a place in the forecast.

Sometimes, "they like us" or "we had a good call" becomes mistaken for buying intent. When qualification questions go unasked or relationship strength is confused for deal momentum, the pipeline fills with false positives.

You can validate deal health by

- Asking, "Who signs the agreement, and have we met them?"
- Probing for customer urgency and the impact if they delay.
- Reviewing whether the rep has mapped the full decision process.

Don't interrogate—coach with curiosity. Inspection should sharpen thinking, not feel like cross-examination.

Progress

Healthy pipelines move. Deals that stall, stall for a reason—and that reason must be uncovered. Progress reviews shine a light on whether opportunities are advancing or quietly expiring.

Be aware of allowing deals to sit idle too long, ignoring close-date slippage, or accepting vague updates like "still in review." These blind spots create inflated forecasts and frustrated teams.

You can track progress by

- Comparing time-in-stage against benchmarks to identify stalled deals.
- Flagging any deal that's slipped twice as "at risk" until progress is proven.
- Asking reps to identify the last customer action, not just their own.

Progress isn't always linear. Some pauses are strategic—great leaders separate legitimate holds from lost momentum.

Evidence

Evidence validates a deal's stage and health. It transforms belief into proof, giving leaders confidence in what's real and what's risky.

Forecasts collapse when deals advance based on optimism or assumptions. Skipping exit criteria or accepting verbal commitments as proof leads to inflated numbers and disappointed leadership calls.

You can strengthen validation by

- Requiring customer-confirmed next steps or documented agreements.
- Using meeting summaries or mutual action plans signed by both sides.
- Asking for written confirmation of the timeline or approval process.

Keep criteria simple and consistent. Overcomplicating validation slows selling—focus on proof that's easy to verify and hard to ignore.

Commit

A true commitment means certainty, not optimism. It's backed by verified sponsor alignment, confirmed timing, and a clear path to signature.

Forecasts lose credibility when reps "commit" deals without confirmed sponsors, overload commits to look good, or carry the same deal forward cycle after cycle. Commitments should reflect confidence, not hope.

You can reinforce the meaning of commitment by

- Accepting commits only when sponsor and process are verified.
- Having reps articulate the exact steps left before close.
- Using mutual close plans that outline the timeline and next actions.

Be strict but fair. Overcommitting kills credibility, but undercommitting hides progress—commit to confidence, not comfort.

Time & Cadence

Forecasts are living systems, not static reports. Cadence builds accuracy and trust; weekly rhythm ensures small problems don't grow into big misses.

Pipeline surprises happen when leaders inspect only at month-end, accept vague updates, or let too much time pass between reviews. A disciplined cadence keeps teams alert and forecasts honest.

You can build rhythm by

- Running a structured weekly cadence: team pipeline → 1:1 inspections → forecast roll-up.
- Tracking week-over-week changes and asking for reasons behind each delta.
- Using a dashboard to visualize trends over time.

Cadence works only if it's consistent. Keep reviews short, specific, and weekly—long, irregular meetings turn inspection into noise.

Note: The INSPECT framework will be expanded in a future mini book within The Seller's Framework series. Visit www.thesellersframework.com for updates and release timelines.

> ### Research Spotlight: Why Forecast Inspection Matters
>
> According to *salesso.com*, 79% of sales organizations miss their forecast by more than 10%.
>
> On the flip side, according to research by *Aberdeen*, 97% of companies that implemented best-in-class forecasting processes achieved quotas, compared to 55% that did not.
>
> Executives view disciplined inspection not as micromanagement but as rigor—a signal that a leader understands their business.

The following week, Jason came prepared.

He started by auditing CRM hygiene—checking every deal for missing amounts, outdated close dates, and empty next-step fields. **(Inputs)**

Then he reviewed his team's coverage numbers, comparing total pipeline to quota and flagging weak conversion stages. **(Numbers)**

In one meeting, he asked Jordan, "You've got five times coverage, but only one deal is past discovery. What's blocking the rest?"

The question forced a deeper discussion about quality over quantity.

Jason began pressing for signals. "Who's signing off on this deal? What happens if they delay?"

Each question pushed reps to verify buyer intent. **(Signals)**

When reviewing progress, he flagged deals that had slipped multiple times. "We've pushed this one twice already. What's different now?"

The conversation turned from excuses to next actions. **(Progress)**

He reinforced the need for evidence—customer emails confirming next meetings, or updated project timelines from client contacts.

"If we can't prove it, we can't forecast it." **(Evidence)**

He redefined commit, removing a few overconfident deals until solid proof was in hand.

"We're going to be accurate before we're optimistic." (**Commit**)

Finally, he set a structured cadence:

- **Mondays:** Team pipeline review
- **Wednesdays:** 1:1 deal inspections
- **Fridays:** Leadership roll-up with clear commentary on every change (**Time & Cadence**)

In the next forecast call, the difference was obvious.

The VP scanned the numbers. "Jason, you've got Maya's deal with Horizon in commit again. Why should I believe it this time?"

Jason met his eyes calmly. "Budget's verified, procurement has reviewed terms, and the client confirmed next steps in writing for Thursday."

The VP nodded. "That's the detail I need."

Maria smiled. Jason's credibility was back—not because of hope, but because of evidence.

He had learned to inspect what he expected.

Chapter 6 Reflection Questions

RESPOND: What's one deal in your current forecast you can inspect for stronger signals and evidence this week?

_____
_____
_____
_____
_____

REFLECT: Are you forecasting based on rep confidence or verified proof?

_____
_____
_____
_____
_____

REPEAT: What inspection cadence will you commit to weekly so your forecasts are consistently credible?

_____
_____
_____
_____
_____

Planning Leadership

"The key is not to prioritize what's on your schedule but to schedule your priorities."

Stephen R. Covey

After being humbled in his first forecast review, Jason realized effort wasn't his problem—organization was.

He'd learned **ORDER** back in Book 1 to run his own day as a rep, but managing was different. Now he had to shape other people's time, priorities, and habits—while still meeting his own obligations.

By his second month, his days were overflowing. His calendar stacked with one-on-ones, leadership updates, deal reviews, and Slack messages that never seemed to stop.

Leadership pressed him to backfill his old position, and interview panels piled on top. He still clung to a few legacy accounts "just to be safe," while the rest of his book had been sliced across the team.

The result was chaos.

In Tuesday's team meeting, there was no agenda—the conversation drifted from lead routing to pricing to a random product bug.

Jason bounced between threads, trying to cover everything and landing nowhere.

Jordan quietly checked his phone. Maya, usually sharp and engaged, went silent.

Alex finally voiced what everyone felt: "These meetings are a waste of selling time."

Outside the meeting, the pattern held. Coaching sessions were rushed or skipped. One-on-ones slid when fires flared.

Tasks kept appearing; priorities kept disappearing.

Jason left each day exhausted, wondering why all his effort wasn't producing momentum.

He was busy—but he wasn't effective.

Aha! Moment

Leadership without prioritization collapses under its own weight. Good intentions won't save you if you can't filter what matters, create structure, and turn motion into momentum.

Maria's Coaching

Maria didn't mince words. "Jason, you're not failing because you don't care. You're failing because you don't have a plan."

"I thought I did," he said. "I'm just trying to keep up."

"Keeping up isn't leading." She paused. "ORDER helped you lead yourself as a rep your prep, your calendar, your calls. But now you're responsible for how others spend their time, how decisions get made, and how work moves. Different problem. Different tools."

She leaned in with questions.

- "What actually matters this week—and how would your calendar prove it?"
- "Which work should stay with you, and which must move to the team so they grow?"
- "How will you structure every interaction so time turns into outcomes?"

- "How will you make sure every conversation ends with visible, owned actions?"

Jason exhaled. "I don't have those answers in a repeatable way."

"Then let's give you one," Maria said. "Use the PLAN framework. It builds on the discipline you learned, but it's designed for managers who must organize people, not just tasks."

The PLAN Framework

Jason didn't need more effort; he needed structure.

PLAN gives new leaders a simple operating system to filter noise, release control, bring shape to meetings and one-on-ones, and convert discussion into action.

Think of it as the bridge between personal productivity and team execution—the discipline that turns an overloaded calendar into consistent outcomes.

Priorities

Focus energy on the few outcomes that move the business. Strong leaders separate the urgent from the important and protect time for the highest-impact work—even when the day gets loud. Priorities should be visible on your calendar, not just in your head.

Many new managers fall into the trap of treating everything as equally urgent, starting the week reactive, and letting other people's agendas drive their time. They confuse busywork—status updates, ad-hoc requests—with the high-leverage work of coaching, hiring, and pipeline quality. Without structure, every ping becomes a fire drill.

You can create focus by

- Defining three weekly outcomes every Monday and blocking calendar time for each before accepting new meetings.
- Tying each priority to a measurable metric (e.g., stage conversion, ramp progress) to avoid vague "do better" goals.
- Sharing your top three in a team channel so alignment is transparent.

Beware the urgent crowding out the important. If your calendar doesn't show time protected for priorities, you don't have priorities—you have intentions.

> ### Sidebar: The Eisenhower Matrix
> 1. Urgent & Important → Do now.
> 2. Important, Not Urgent → Schedule and protect.
> 3. Urgent, Not Important → Delegate when possible.
> 4. Neither → Eliminate.
>
> Great leaders spend most of their time in Quadrant 2: important but not urgent.

Lean on Others

Leadership multiplies when work is distributed with clarity. Delegation grows capability and frees you to focus on higher-order priorities like coaching, hiring, and strategy. Done right, it increases quality and speed because more people are learning to lead.

Managers weaken their impact when they hoard legacy accounts, delegate without defining outcomes, or practice "drive-by delegation"—dropping tasks without context or support. Real delegation transfers ownership and builds confidence.

You can delegate effectively by

- Using a handoff checklist that outlines the owner, goal, milestones, risks, and first review date.
- Assigning a rep to own a portion of the team meeting—prep together, then debrief for growth.
- Transitioning your last two legacy accounts with a 30/60/90-day plan.

Don't outsource leadership decisions, but do release execution that develops your people. Delegation without clarity becomes abdication; clarity turns it into development.

Agenda

Agendas turn time into progress. They give meetings shape, purpose, and accountability. A clear agenda frames decisions, limits drift, and makes space for voices that might otherwise be drowned out.

Meetings lose value when leaders run them without structure, use them for information that could've been a pre-read, or allow sidebars to hijack focus. A light, purposeful agenda prevents "update theater" and keeps discussions moving toward outcomes.

You can lead better meetings by

- Pre-sharing a three-point agenda with timeboxes and desired outcomes (e.g., "decide," "align," "brainstorm").
- Starting with the decision to be made and ending each section with the decision captured.
- Parking off-topic items in a visible list and assigning owners for follow-up.

Agendas shouldn't suffocate discussion. Build in space for real issues—but never show up without a clear purpose and path.

Next Steps

Clarity closes the loop. Every interaction should end with who owns what by when, captured where everyone can see it. Next steps convert talk into traction and create a natural rhythm for accountability.

Many leaders end meetings with vague commitments like "Let's follow up later" or "Sounds good," leaving action items invisible or forgotten. When responsibilities stay in someone's head instead of a shared tracker, execution collapses into chaos.

You can build follow-through by

- Closing each meeting by reading out action items into a shared tracker (e.g., "Maya → 25-logo target list by Fri 4 PM; Jordan → draft outreach script by Thu noon; Jason → escalate enablement request by Wed EOD").
- Sending a three-bullet recap within 30 minutes summarizing decisions, owners, and deadlines.

- Starting the next meeting by reviewing last week's commitments before tackling new topics.

If it isn't written and owned, it doesn't exist. Make actions visible and time-bound so follow-through becomes habit—not heroics.

Note: The PLAN framework will be expanded in a future mini book within The Seller's Framework series. For updates and release timelines, visit www.thesellersframework.com.

> ### Research Spotlight: Why PLAN Stops the Chaos
> Managers rarely fail from a lack of effort; they fail from a lack of organization. Research shows that high role clarity significantly results in higher job satisfaction and lower turnover rates. PLAN gives leaders a practical operating system across the week: set Priorities, Lean on others with clarity, bring Agendas to every interaction, and close with visible Next Steps that create momentum.

That Monday, Jason applied **PLAN** everywhere—down with his team, across with peers, and up with leadership.

At 8:00 a.m., he wrote three outcomes on his whiteboard and blocked time for each: improve stage-2→3 conversion, finish backfill interview loop, and stand up a weekly coaching cadence.

He declined two ad-hoc meetings that didn't map to those outcomes and posted his priorities in the team channel. (**Priorities**)

He finally released his last two legacy accounts.

"Maya, you own NorthBridge—here's the handoff doc with milestones and risks; I'll review progress with you next Wednesday."

To Jordan: "You'll run the pipeline segment of Friday's team meeting; I'll help you prep Thursday." (**Lean on Others**)

He sent the team meeting agenda early:

1. Decide outreach focus for strategic logos.
2. Align on comp-plan outreach messaging.
3. Review two stuck deals and choose next actions.

A parking lot captured side issues without derailing. (**Agenda**)

At the end, he said, "Let's read out actions." (**Next Steps**)

"Maya—build a target list of 25 enterprise logos and first-touch plan by Friday 4 p.m."

"Jordan—draft the comp-plan outreach script by Thursday noon; I'll redline it by 3 p.m."

"Jason—submit enablement request to ops for the battlecard updates by Wednesday EOD."

He pasted the list into the shared tracker and sent a three-bullet recap within 20 minutes.

At their next huddle, he opened by reviewing last week's commitments before new topics.

In his one-on-one with Jordan, he didn't rattle off metrics. "What pattern do you see here?"

Jordan noticed his call-to-meeting drop-off and proposed a new first-call structure.

"Own it," Jason said. "Send me your draft by Thursday, and we'll test it next week."

And in his leadership update, Jason arrived with a crisp agenda, three priorities, and visible team actions with owners and dates.

The conversation was faster and sharper.

Maria smiled. "You're making my job easier."

Jason walked out realizing **PLAN** worked.

Organization wasn't a flavor of the week—it was how he'd lead, consistently. But getting organized was only half the job; now he had to carry leadership's message without losing his team.

Chapter 7 Reflection Questions

RESPOND: What one priority will you clarify and protect on your calendar this week?

_____
_____
_____
_____
_____

REFLECT: Where are you still holding onto work you should transfer to grow your team?

_____
_____
_____
_____
_____

REPEAT: What meeting rhythm or agenda habit will you commit to so clarity becomes part of your leadership identity?

_____
_____
_____
_____
_____

Manager in the Middle

*"Leadership is not about being in charge.
It is about taking care of those in your charge."*

Simon Sinek

CHAPTER EIGHT

Jason was finally beginning to feel the relief of **PLAN**. Meetings had agendas, coaching had rhythm, and his days felt less chaotic. For the first time in weeks, he sensed progress.

He had also begun applying **INSPECT** with his team, and leadership was starting to trust his forecasts.

Then came the email from his VP.

A new compensation plan had been announced, designed to push larger, more strategic deals.

Jason was tasked with rolling it out to the team.

Still finding his footing as a manager, he decided the safest move was to deliver the message exactly as he received it—top-down, word for word.

The reaction was immediate.

Alex leaned back in his chair, smirking. "Of course leadership wants us to do more with less. Nothing new there."

Maya frowned, clearly worried about the added pressure.

Samantha crossed her arms, visibly frustrated.

Jordan, the newest hire, looked especially unsettled. "Wait...so the plan I was hired under is already changing?"

Jason felt his stomach tighten. He wanted to empathize but instead defaulted to defending.

"Look, this is what leadership wants. We just have to make it work."

The team left discouraged, muttering among themselves.

Jason walked out feeling caught between two fires—pressure from above, resistance from below.

He realized he hadn't led; he'd simply passed along a message.

Aha! Moment

Passing messages down without context erodes trust. Middle managers must bridge, not parrot. That means listening, translating, and involving so both leadership and the team see them as credible.

Maria's Coaching

Later that week, Jason vented in Maria's office.

"I feel stuck. Leadership expects me to sell this plan, but the team doesn't buy in. No matter what I say, Alex shoots it down, and everyone else piles on."

Maria leaned forward. "Jason, what role does Alex play in how the team reacts?"

Jason sighed. "A big one. They watch him. If he resists, they follow."

"Right. Did you give the team a chance to voice concerns before you defended the change?"

"No... I just rolled it out as is."

"And did you connect the plan to what it means for them—not just for the company?"

Jason frowned. "I don't think I did."

Maria nodded. "Balancing up and down isn't about choosing sides—it's about translating. You have to empathize with the team while aligning with leadership. Invite input, frame the why, and involve even the skeptics. That's how you bridge both directions."

Jason looked up. "So, how do I actually do that?"

Maria smiled. "Use the **BRIDGE** framework. It builds on the **ORDER** you learned as a rep and the structure of **PLAN**, but it's different—you're now translating strategy between two levels. That's the real test of leadership."

The BRIDGE Framework

Being a "manager in the middle" means living between competing pressures—executive expectations above and team realities below. Great managers don't just repeat messages; they interpret them. The BRIDGE framework helps leaders connect both directions with credibility, trust, and clarity.

Brief the Why

Every communication should begin with context. Anchoring messages in both company growth and team benefit transforms compliance into understanding. When people know why a decision matters—to the business and to them—resistance drops and engagement rises.

Leaders lose credibility when they over-explain, share only corporate goals, or present mandatory changes as optional. Clarity builds confidence; defensiveness erodes it.

You can build stronger alignment by

- Explaining why the change matters organizationally and personally.
- Linking the shift to long-term team or career benefits, not just top-line metrics.
- Stating desired outcomes clearly so everyone understands the win.

Be clear but concise. State the why, then invite questions—don't over-defend it.

Reflect Concerns

Before solving, acknowledge. Reflection validates emotions and builds trust. The ability to say "I hear you" sincerely—even when you can't alter the decision—earns far more credibility than trying to argue someone into agreement.

When leaders ignore pushback, counter emotion with logic, or take resistance personally–it closes ears and hardens opinions. Reflection creates space for perspective and calm.

You can strengthen trust by

- Naming how the change might feel for the team.
- Paraphrasing key concerns before offering any response.
- Validating emotion even when you don't share the conclusion.

Recognition isn't agreement. Validation opens ears faster than defense ever will.

Involve Key Voices

Critics and influencers shape perception. Involving them early—by asking for their insight and inviting observations—turns potential resistance into engagement. Involvement isn't about seeking approval; it's about ensuring people feel heard and that their feedback sharpens execution.

Avoiding skeptics, relying only on enthusiastic voices, or asking for feedback you never act on all weaken credibility. Inclusive communication creates ownership.

You can involve others effectively by

- Asking team members what challenges they anticipate and what support would help.
- Running short follow-ups after rollout to capture patterns in feedback.
- Recognizing thoughtful, evidence-based input publicly.

Involve skeptics, but set boundaries. Ask for insight—not permission—and you'll build respect across the spectrum.

Define the Message

Simplify and translate. Defining the message means turning broad strategy into "what this means for us." A leader's job is to make direction practical—clear roles, behaviors, and next steps that convert vision into motion.

When managers repeat corporate jargon, drown people in detail, or skip expectations altogether, the message gets lost in noise. Clarity isn't dilution—it's precision.

You can bring clarity by

- Boiling updates into two or three plain-language takeaways tied to team actions.
- Replacing buzzwords with examples your team recognizes.
- Ending each communication with "who does what by when."

Translate, don't twist. Keep leadership's intent intact while making it actionable and memorable.

Ground in Evidence

Evidence turns theory into credibility. It explains why now and supports the change with proof. When managers connect messages to data, results, or external trends, they transform opinion into confidence.

Many leaders rely on vague assurances—"leadership says this works"—or skip data entirely, leaving teams to question motive and method. The best communicators back their story with proof.

You can reinforce credibility by

- Sharing results from pilots or comparable teams that achieved measurable gains.
- Referencing customer or market trends that support the timing.
- Showing before-and-after snapshots that make the impact visible.

Be specific, not exhaustive. Choose the few data points that most effectively support your case.

Escalate Upward

Feedback flows both ways. Escalating upward isn't venting—it's informing. It means synthesizing what you're hearing into patterns, evidence-backed insights, and practical recommendations that help senior leaders make better decisions.

When managers either protect leadership from bad news or pass along every complaint verbatim, it erodes trust. Leaders who summarize with context and balance become credible conduits between levels.

You can elevate insight by

- Summarizing recurring concerns and backing them with examples or data.
- Highlighting potential business impacts like risk to cycle time or enablement needs.
- Pairing each theme with a suggested adjustment or solution.

Escalate facts, not noise. Focus on patterns, impacts, and options leadership can act on.

Research Spotlight:
Why Middle Managers Must Bridge Both Ways

Harvard Business Review calls middle managers the "linchpins" of every organization—translating strategy downward and surfacing insight upward.

> *McKinsey* research shows companies that actively equip their middle layer to connect executive vision with frontline reality are far more effective at executing change.
>
> Change-management studies confirm resistance drops dramatically when managers both explain the "why" and invite input, proving that translation, not repetition, drives adoption.

At the next team meeting, Jason approached the same compensation plan differently.

"I know changes like this can feel disruptive," he began. "Some of you are probably frustrated or worried. That's fair, and I hear you." (**Reflect**)

He paused, letting the tension settle before continuing.

"Here's what leadership's asking: they want us focused on larger, more strategic deals because it positions the company for growth. For us, that means fewer closes to hit quota and bigger wins when we land them." (**Brief**)

Then he clarified what that meant in practical terms.

"For our team, this comes down to three things: shifting outreach toward larger accounts, collaborating more deeply on strategy, and celebrating the bigger wins we secure together." (**Define**)

Jason didn't stop there—he invited engagement.

"What adjustments do you think we need to make to target these accounts effectively?"

Maya suggested mapping key enterprise clients; Jordan proposed partnering with marketing for stronger outreach.

Even Alex, though skeptical, raised valid concerns about deal cycle length. (**Involve**)

Jason acknowledged their input and grounded it in results.

"Those are fair points. The two biggest wins we had last quarter came from accounts just like these—where we focused on strategy early and stayed consistent through the process. When we focus there, we're building on proven momentum." (**Ground**)

He wrapped up by promising to carry their feedback upward.

"I'll take your points about cycle timing and lead support to leadership so they understand what it takes to execute this successfully." (**Escalate**)

The room felt different this time.

The plan hadn't changed, but how it was delivered had.

The team left feeling heard, not handed down to. They understood both the *why* behind leadership's decision and the *how* of their role in it.

Jason realized he hadn't erased all discomfort—but he had replaced resistance with clarity and trust.

Chapter 8 Reflection Questions

RESPOND: What one leadership message do you need to translate for my team this week, not just repeat?

_____
_____
_____
_____
_____

REFLECT: Do you tend to defend leadership too quickly or side with the team too easily?

_____
_____
_____
_____
_____

REPEAT: How will you use BRIDGE regularly so both leadership and your team see you as credible?

_____
_____
_____
_____
_____

Subscribe Today!

If you're enjoying *From Seller to Sales Leader*, please subscribe to *The Seller's Framework* newsletter for new book releases, sales resources, and more!

https://www.thesellersframework.com/home#subscribe

The Seller's Framework Newsletter

Coaching with Consistency

"Consistency is the true foundation of trust. Either keep your promises, or do not make them."

Roy T. Bennett

CHAPTER NINE

Jason started the week the way most new managers do—determined to do it right.

His calendar looked perfect on Monday morning: one-on-ones blocked, team huddles scheduled, prep time carved out. He promised himself that this would be the week he stayed disciplined.

Then reality hit.

A client escalated a pricing issue. Leadership moved up a forecast review.

Slack buzzed nonstop with messages from reps needing answers now.

His phone lit up with side requests, questions, and updates from every direction.

By Wednesday, the first one-on-one was rescheduled. By Friday, another was shortened to ten rushed minutes between calls. What had started as structure quickly slid back into chaos.

Jordan felt supported one week but forgotten the next. Maya stayed quiet but noticed the inconsistency. Samantha took it personally. "Guess my growth isn't a priority."

And Alex, always the cynic, shrugged. "Told you, these meetings never last."

Jason didn't mean to neglect anyone—he was just overwhelmed. But inconsistency was sending a message louder than his words: their development was negotiable.

Aha! Moment

Coaching gains power not from intensity, but from rhythm. Trust isn't built by great conversations—it's built by predictable ones.

Maria's Coaching

Jason admitted his frustration. "I want to coach, but there's always something urgent. And honestly, half the team doesn't even want it."

Maria leaned back. "Jason, what message do you think you send when you cancel a one-on-one?"

Jason exhaled. "That they're not a priority."

"Exactly. Coaching isn't an event, it's a rhythm. When you keep that rhythm, people learn to trust that growth matters here. Show up consistently, prepare intentionally, and expect your reps to do the same. Rhythm plus intent builds accountability."

The CONSIST Framework

In Book 1, Jason learned the COACH framework—how to structure a single conversation for growth.

Now, as a leader, he must master CONSIST—how to sustain that rhythm week after week.

If COACH is the skill, CONSIST is the system that makes the skill stick.

Coaching has the greatest impact when it's both consistent and intentional. The CONSIST framework helps leaders turn coaching from a good intention into a dependable operating rhythm.

Cadence

Consistency builds credibility. Protect recurring one-on-ones as non-negotiable calendar anchors. A steady cadence signals that development isn't a luxury—it's part of the job. When coaching time becomes predictable, performance conversations move from reactive to proactive.

Be cautious to cancel or move sessions when something "more important" appears, hold one-on-ones irregularly, or treat coaching as optional for high performers. Those patterns communicate that growth is secondary to urgency.

You can create reliability by

- Holding coaching at the same day and time each week.
- Rescheduling within 24 hours when conflicts arise.
- Keeping frequency equal for every rep, not just those struggling.

Keep cadence steady but flexible. Adjust for emergencies, not convenience—rhythm matters more than perfection.

Observe

Real coaching is grounded in reality. Observation transforms opinion into insight. Whether shadowing a live call or reviewing a recording, you learn what truly drives or blocks performance—and can coach behavior, not hearsay.

When managers coach only from reports or CRM notes, they miss the nuances of tone, pacing, and presence that shape results. Feedback without firsthand evidence often feels detached or unfair.

You can build observation into your rhythm by

- Reviewing one recorded call per rep each week.
- Joining a live meeting and debriefing immediately afterward.
- Using short call snippets to highlight best practices in team huddles.

Observe to support, not to surveil. Make observation feel developmental, not disciplinary.

Notes & Preparation

Preparation shows respect. When both leader and rep arrive prepared, coaching becomes focused and meaningful. Document insights, questions, and next steps to turn growth into continuity instead of repetition.

Coaching falters when leaders walk in unprepared, rely on memory, or dominate the conversation. Structure prevents drift and keeps the focus on progress.

You can stay prepared by

- Keeping a running log of commitments and progress for each rep.
- Asking reps to bring one area they want to improve.
- Starting sessions by reviewing last week's goals.

Avoid over-prepping. The goal is focus and flow, not paperwork.

Shared Ownership

Coaching is collaboration, not command. When reps co-create next steps, they commit more fully and follow through faster. Shared ownership turns passive listeners into active learners and builds lasting accountability.

Leaders weaken development when they lecture, solve every problem, or accept silent agreement. Growth sticks when the rep helps shape the plan.

You can foster ownership by

- Asking, "What will you try differently next time?"
- Letting reps summarize their own takeaways.
- Ending each session with one clear action owned by the rep.

Guide, don't dictate. Ownership means shared commitment—not abdication.

Informal Access

Growth happens between sessions. Informal touchpoints—quick check-ins, encouragement, or spontaneous feedback—show that coaching isn't confined to the calendar. Approachability reinforces trust and continuity.

When leaders only engage during scheduled meetings or reach out only when problems arise, they send the signal that coaching equals correction. Informal access reminds people that development is ongoing.

You can stay connected by

- Sending short praise messages after observed progress.
- Offering a quick debrief during hallway chats or ride-alongs.
- Asking midweek, "What's working best right now?"

Stay available without hovering. Informal access strengthens trust but never replaces structured sessions.

Small Wins

Momentum is built one step at a time. Recognizing small wins reinforces effort, builds confidence, and motivates continued improvement.

Leaders who celebrate only big outcomes—or focus solely on what's missing—miss countless moments to encourage progress. Recognition, when specific and timely, accelerates development.

You can reinforce progress by

- Publicly celebrating one improvement per rep each week.
- Highlighting positive changes during team huddles.
- Giving concrete praise: "Your pacing on that demo showed real control."

Celebrate growth while maintaining standards. Recognition should inspire performance, not excuse mediocrity.

Track Progress

What gets tracked gets repeated. Visible tracking creates shared accountability and helps both leader and rep see progress over time.

It transforms coaching from a series of conversations into a measurable journey.

When goals are forgotten or improvement isn't documented, coaching loses continuity. A simple tracking system keeps momentum visible and connects development directly to outcomes.

You can maintain traction by

- Logging goals, actions, and results in a simple shared tracker.
- Opening each session by reviewing last week's commitments.
- Using quarterly summaries to highlight long-term growth trends.

Tracking should encourage, not control. Use it to inspire follow-through, not to micromanage.

Research Spotlight: Why Consistency Matters

According to the *2022 State of Sales Training and Onboarding* report by *Spekit*, 65% of top performers tie their success to regular coaching and real-time feedback.

CSO Insights (2019) listed coaching effectiveness as a top predictor of sales success—but only when it's consistent.

Gallup (2019) showed that managers who make themselves available for informal coaching drive higher engagement and retention.

ATD confirmed that tracking progress boosts skill adoption by 70 percent.

> Consistency transforms effort into trust—and trust into performance.

Jason decided to reset—not start over, but return to discipline. Coaching would no longer be something he "fit in." It would be the structure his week revolved around.

He blocked recurring one-on-ones for every rep and treated them as sacred, rescheduling within 24 hours if conflicts arose. (**Cadence**)

He spent part of each Monday reviewing call recordings and shadowed several live meetings, taking notes on tone, pacing, and engagement so his feedback came from firsthand observation. (**Observe**)

Before each session, he reviewed last week's notes and opened with, "What's one area you want to focus on today?" The shared agenda made coaching more purposeful. (**Notes & Preparation**)

He ended each meeting with a single action item owned by the rep, logging it in his tracker and confirming next steps together. (**Shared Ownership**)

During the week, he sent quick check-ins and short encouragements after good calls, reinforcing effort in real time. (**Informal Access**)

He recognized improvements in team huddles, spotlighting how small behaviors—better discovery questions, cleaner recaps—were compounding into results. (**Small Wins**)

Every Friday, he reviewed the tracker, noting completed actions and trends, then shared one progress highlight with the team. (**Track Progress**)

Over the next several weeks, Jason's rhythm took root. Coaching became expected, not optional. The team trusted that feedback would come regularly, not sporadically. Even Alex stopped rolling his eyes—because Jason always showed up.

Chapter 9 Reflection Questions

RESPOND: What's one action you can take this week to make coaching a consistent rhythm?

_____
_____
_____
_____
_____

REFLECT: How does your consistency, or lack of it, affect your team's trust in you as a leader?

_____
_____
_____
_____
_____

REPEAT: What system will you use to track coaching progress so growth becomes visible over time?

_____
_____
_____
_____
_____

Accountability and Performance Gaps

"When there is no accountability, there is no performance."

Patrick Lencioni

CHAPTER TEN

Jason stared at the quarterly report, jaw tight. His team was close to hitting the goal, except for one glaring miss: Samantha.

She'd fallen short of quota by nearly 20%, and it wasn't a one-time dip. Over the past six weeks, she'd missed key follow-ups, let two proposals expire, and dropped a client renewal that had been projected to close. Those small misses had now compounded into a significant shortfall.

Jason had seen it coming. He'd noticed the declining activity, the disengaged tone in meetings, and the quiet frustration behind her polite nods. Each time he considered raising it, he talked himself out of it. "She's capable," he reasoned. "She just needs space to rebound."

But now, the numbers weren't just hurting her; they were hurting the team. Jordan had picked up one of her dropped accounts, Maya was carrying extra client calls, and even Alex had started whispering about "double standards." Jason felt the weight of leadership pressing down. His silence had turned from empathy into avoidance.

Aha! Moment

Avoiding accountability doesn't preserve trust; it erodes it. Leaders earn respect when they address performance gaps directly, clearly, and with care.

Maria's Coaching

Jason sat across from Maria, his expression conflicted.

"She's missed quota again," he said. "I've brought it up in passing, but I haven't had a real talk. I don't want her to feel attacked."

Maria folded her hands. "Jason, accountability isn't about attacking—it's about alignment. You're not calling her out; you're calling her up. It's holding someone to a standard, helping them achieve it, and showing your team that those standards apply to everyone."

Jason exhaled slowly. "I just don't want to damage trust."

Maria leaned forward. "Jason, that's exactly how you build it. When you avoid accountability, you tell the team effort and results are optional. When you address it fairly, you tell them you care enough to help them succeed."

He nodded, quietly realizing that silence had said more than he intended.

The CLEAR Framework

Accountability isn't confrontation—it's clarity plus care. The CLEAR framework helps leaders address performance gaps with structure, empathy, and follow-through.

When applied well, CLEAR transforms accountability from an uncomfortable task into a culture of ownership. It ensures expectations are known, performance is discussed early, and progress is measured fairly. Leaders who use CLEAR don't just correct—they develop.

Clarify the Gap

Clarity brings fairness. Accountability starts with identifying the precise gap between expectations and outcomes—in behavior, numbers, or follow-through. Use data and specifics, not assumptions or emotion. When the problem is clear, both sides can focus on solutions instead of blame.

Be careful to assume reps already know they're missing the mark, give vague feedback like "you need to step it up," or let frustration cloud their message. Specificity turns discomfort into direction.

You can clarify effectively by

- Saying, "Your quarterly target was $250K; you closed $195K."
- Noting, "Two renewal follow-ups went past due, which delayed client decisions."
- Outlining, "You committed to six demos per week but averaged three."

Stick to what's observable and measurable. Clarity removes emotion and opens the door for honest conversation.

Listen to Understand

Before diagnosing, understand. Listening means giving space for context—the person's story, challenges, and perspective. It shows empathy and reinforces that accountability is about partnership, not punishment. When people feel heard, they engage more openly in solving the problem.

Many managers rush to correction, interrupt explanations, or assume they already know why performance slipped. That approach breeds defensiveness instead of dialogue.

You can listen with intent by

- Asking, "What's felt most challenging for you this quarter?"
- Exploring, "Where do you feel things started to slip?"
- Checking, "What obstacles are keeping you from consistent follow-up?"

Empathy doesn't erase accountability. Understanding the person is step one; holding them to the standard is step two.

Examine Root Causes

Understanding alone isn't enough—you must diagnose accurately. Examine what's truly causing the gap: is it a skill issue (can't), a will issue (won't), or a clarity issue (don't know how)? By analyzing evidence, not emotion, you coach the right problem and avoid wasted effort.

Be careful to treat every issue as a motivation problem or fix surface symptoms without addressing underlying behaviors. True improvement requires insight, not assumption.

You can examine effectively by

- Reviewing pipeline data to see where deals consistently stall.
- Listening to call recordings to identify skill breakdowns.
- Comparing activity levels to find consistency drops.

Focus on evidence, not emotion. Diagnosis leads to progress when it targets the real barrier, not the visible symptom.

Agree on Actions

Awareness must lead to action. Work with the rep to co-create clear, measurable, time-bound steps for improvement. Collaboration turns correction into commitment and ensures accountability is done with them, not to them.

Leaders dilute impact when they dictate instructions, give vague goals like "do better next month," or fail to define ownership and deadlines. Specificity and shared authorship drive follow-through.

You can build ownership by

- Setting, "You'll complete five prospecting blocks weekly for the next three weeks."
- Planning, "We'll debrief two calls per week to track progress and confidence."
- Committing, "You'll send post-call recaps within 24 hours to strengthen follow-through."

Document it. If it's not written down, it won't be tracked—and what isn't tracked rarely changes.

Reinforce Consistency

Accountability becomes culture through repetition. Following up weekly or biweekly, celebrating progress, and addressing slippage early communicates that development matters every day, not just when performance dips.

Leaders who only check in after problems reappear or ignore small wins miss their chance to reinforce the right habits. Consistent follow-through proves that accountability equals support.

You can reinforce effectively by

- Opening one-on-ones by revisiting prior commitments.
- Publicly recognizing effort that's moving the needle.
- Re-addressing small lapses quickly before they widen.

Hold everyone to the same standard. Consistency builds credibility, and credibility builds trust.

> ### Research Spotlight: Why Accountability Builds Trust
>
> *Gallup* (2022) found that only 26% of employees strongly agree that feedback improves performance, largely due to inconsistency and vagueness.
>
> Teams with structured accountability rhythms are more likely to exceed quota and be more engaged. Accountability done well isn't punishment—it's partnership rooted in clarity, fairness, and consistency.

Jason scheduled a private meeting with Samantha the following morning.

"Samantha," he began, keeping his tone calm and professional, "I want to talk through where things stand. Your quarterly goal was $250K, and you closed $195K. We also had a couple of renewals and proposals slip, including the Grant account. What do you think contributed most to that gap?" (**Clarify the Gap**)

Samantha shifted in her chair. "Honestly, I'm not sure. The larger deals have been harder to move forward, and I've been putting more time into smaller ones just to get something going."

Jason nodded slowly. "That makes sense. When you think about those larger deals, what's been making them harder?" (**Listen to Understand**)

She thought for a moment. "They take longer to build momentum, and I don't always know who to reach out to next. I guess I get discouraged and go back to what feels easier."

Jason leaned forward slightly. "So part of it might be confidence in navigating those larger accounts?" (**Examine Root Causes**)

"Yeah," she admitted. "That, and I've been managing my time poorly. I start the week strong but get distracted midweek."

Jason smiled encouragingly. "That's helpful. What do you think would help you rebuild consistency and confidence with those accounts?"

Samantha considered it. "Maybe I could block out specific prospecting time for larger accounts—and stick to it, no matter what."

Jason nodded. "That's a great start. How much time feels realistic to protect each week?" (**Agree on Actions**)

"Two focused blocks," she said. "And I could bring one of those account conversations to our one-on-one for review."

"Perfect," Jason replied. "Let's try that for the next three weeks and track progress together. I'll check in during our Friday one-on-ones, and we'll look for small wins along the way." (**Reinforce Consistency**)

Samantha exhaled, visibly relieved. "Thank you. This actually feels doable. I just needed to talk it through."

Jason smiled. "That's the goal. You have what it takes, Samantha; this is just about getting you back into rhythm."

Over the next few weeks, Samantha followed through on the plan.

Her outreach improved, her tone in calls grew more confident, and her activity became steady again.

She wasn't at quota yet, but she was trending upward—and most importantly, she was taking ownership of her improvement.

Jason realized accountability wasn't about directing performance—it was about guiding ownership.

Chapter 10 Reflection Questions

RESPOND: Which performance issue on your team requires clarity and care this week?

REFLECT: Does your accountability conversations balance empathy with evidence?

REPEAT: How can you build a rhythm of follow-up that turns accountability into culture?

Cross-Department Collaboration

*"Alone we can do so little,
but together we can do so much."*

Helen Keller

Jason's team was finally gaining traction.

Deals were moving, forecasts were cleaner, and one-on-ones had rhythm again.

But just as his internal house came together, new friction appeared—this time from the departments around him.

The complaints started small but grew louder.

"Marketing's leads are garbage," Maya muttered, scrolling through unresponsive prospects.

"Customer Success takes forever to follow up," Jordan said, exasperated.

"Ops keeps killing my deals with their pricing model," Alex grumbled, tossing his pen on the desk.

Jason felt the pressure mounting. He wanted to defend his team—after all, their frustrations weren't entirely wrong.

But instead of coaching them toward solutions, he absorbed their irritation and carried it into his own conversations with peers.

In his next leadership sync, his comments came out sharper than intended.

He told Marketing their leads weren't converting and accused Operations of blocking deals with pricing rules.

When he met with Customer Success, he pressed them to "speed things up" without understanding their workload.

What he saw as advocacy landed as accusation.

Peers bristled. Silos hardened.

And word spread quickly: "Jason doesn't get how other departments operate."

By the time Maria heard the feedback, Jason's credibility outside his team had started to erode.

Aha! Moment

Collaboration breaks down when leaders carry frustration instead of creating connection. You can't build trust by relaying complaints—only by translating them into shared understanding.

Maria's Coaching

Jason slumped into Maria's office, frustration visible on his face.

"It feels like every department is making our jobs harder. Marketing sends junk leads, Customer Success drags their feet, and Operations won't budge on pricing. My team's fed up, and honestly, so am I."

Maria listened carefully before responding. "I get it, Jason. The frustration is real, and it's okay to feel it. But here's where leadership changes the rules—emotion can't be the loudest voice in the room."

Jason looked up. "So I shouldn't say anything?"

Maria shook her head. "You should. But not before reflection. Your reps don't get a free pass to vent either. You need to coach them through the same process I'm coaching you through: reflect before reacting. Ask, What's emotion? What's evidence? What's within our control?"

Jason nodded slowly. "So I coach them through ownership first—and then model it when I talk with other leaders."

"Exactly," Maria said. "When you walk across the hall, you don't echo frustration—you elevate it. You represent your team's perspective with credibility and curiosity. That's how you **LINK**: Listen first, Identify shared goals, Navigate differences, and Keep aligned. It's how leaders turn friction into partnership."

The LINK Framework

Cross-department collaboration is where good managers either earn influence or lose it. You can be respected within your own team yet lose credibility the moment you speak to another function. LINK provides a structure to turn competing priorities into shared progress.

It's not about softening your message—it's about strengthening it with context, curiosity, and consistency.

Listen First

Listening is about connection first, not concession. Start by asking questions that uncover what matters most to the other team—their goals, challenges, and measures of success. When you lead with curiosity, you replace defensiveness with openness and demonstrate genuine respect for their priorities.

Many leaders make the mistake of leading with frustration, interrupting, or assuming they already understand another team's pressures. That approach creates tension instead of trust.

You can open collaboration by

- Asking, "What's your top priority this quarter?"
- Exploring, "What challenges are you up against that I might not see?"
- Clarifying, "What does success look like from your side?"

Listening doesn't mean agreeing—it means understanding before responding, building the foundation for real collaboration.

Identify Shared Goals

Alignment begins when both sides see a common win. Identifying shared goals creates purpose beyond departmental walls—linking efforts to outcomes that benefit everyone. When teams share ownership of results like revenue growth, efficiency, or customer experience, tension gives way to partnership.

Collaboration breaks down when conversations focus only on one side's needs, assume alignment without confirmation, or revolve around emotions instead of business outcomes. Shared goals must be visible and measurable.

You can build alignment by

- Connecting outcomes: "If we can raise lead quality, both conversion and campaign ROI improve."
- Bridging priorities: "You want smoother onboarding; we want better retention. Let's connect those."
- Finding overlap: "We're both chasing customer satisfaction—how can we simplify the handoff?"

Keep shared goals tied to measurable impact. They only hold weight when they move business results, not personal preferences.

Navigate Differences

Differences are inevitable—but they don't have to divide. Navigating means addressing friction with respect, searching for solutions instead of fault. True collaboration manages tension productively, balancing trade-offs in a way that moves both teams forward.

Leaders often avoid hard conversations to "keep the peace," escalate too quickly, or treat disagreement as opposition. In reality, healthy debate sharpens outcomes when handled with skill and composure.

You can navigate effectively by

- Asking, "Our timelines conflict. What can each of us adjust to stay aligned?"
- Balancing constraints: "Margins are tight, but here's what the client expects. Where's the flexibility?"
- Framing resolution: "Before we decide, let's map what success looks like for both."

The goal isn't to win the argument—it's to advance the business.

Keep Aligned

Alignment isn't a one-time event; it's a continuous process. Sustaining it requires rhythm—recurring check-ins, shared visibility, and proactive updates. When teams stay connected, misunderstandings shrink and collaboration strengthens.

Avoid assuming one meeting creates lasting agreement, rely on hallway conversations, or let early momentum fade for lack of structure. Real alignment is maintained through consistency.

You can keep collaboration strong by

- Hosting monthly cross-functional syncs with documented next steps.
- Sending quick follow-up summaries to capture agreements.
- Maintaining shared dashboards visible to both teams.

Alignment fades without maintenance. Protect it through consistent rhythms and transparent communication.

> **Research Spotlight: Why Collaboration Matters**
>
> Organizations with strong cross-department collaboration are significantly more likely to achieve high performance. *Harvard Business Review* adds that credibility grows when leaders balance advocacy for their team with empathy for others. Collaboration isn't about pleasing everyone—it's about connecting perspectives to move the business forward.

Jason started inside his own team.

When frustrations flared, he paused them with questions instead of agreeing.

"Okay, Maya—if the leads feel unqualified, what would make them stronger? Let's figure out what we can do differently before we take it to Marketing."

When Jordan complained about delays, Jason asked, "How can we set better client expectations so Customer Success has time to follow through?"

Gradually, the team stopped venting and started problem-solving.

Then Jason took that same mindset outward.

With Marketing, he began differently.

"Can you walk me through your current campaign goals this quarter?" he asked.

Marketing shared their focus on awareness.

Jason nodded. "That helps. If we refine how leads are scored before handoff, we'll see faster engagement—that benefits both of us." (**Listen, Identify**)

With Customer Success, he approached with empathy.

"I know your backlog is heavy," he said. "But we both care about client retention. If we coordinate earlier in the process, can that ease the load on your team and keep deals moving?" (**Navigate**)

With Operations, he came prepared.

"I understand the margin constraints," he said. "But here's how current pricing affects client urgency. What would it take to pilot a few flexible options?"

Together, they launched a short test plan and agreed to review the impact monthly. (**Keep Aligned**)

Over the next few weeks, Jason noticed a shift.

His team was calmer, more focused, and peers were reaching out to collaborate instead of defend.

He hadn't silenced frustrations—he'd translated them into progress.

Collaboration wasn't about avoiding tension

Chapter 11 Reflection Questions

RESPOND: Which department relationship do you need to listen to and align with more intentionally this week?

_____

_____

_____

_____

REFLECT: How often are you carrying complaints across the hall instead of coaching reps toward ownership?

_____

_____

_____

_____

REPEAT: What rhythm (check-ins, shared dashboards, ongoing communication) can you set to keep cross-department alignment strong?

_____

_____

_____

_____

Performance Plans

"The standard you walk past is the standard you accept."

General David Hurley

CHAPTER TWELVE

A little over four months into Jason's leadership, the cracks had become visible.

Samantha had now missed quota for the third consecutive month. Earlier, they had created an accountability plan together—increased outreach, better preparation, and improved follow-up—but the results hadn't materialized.

Client meetings remained inconsistent, follow-ups slipped, and proposals were sent late. Two prospects even went cold after missed deadlines, costing the team both revenue and trust. Samantha arrived late to meetings and often seemed distracted.

Jason saw the warning signs but hesitated again. "It's been a tough quarter," he told her gently. "I know you'll turn it around." He meant to encourage her, but instead, he let the issue linger.

The longer he waited, the worse it got. Jordan quietly wondered why standards seemed different for some people. Maya, who had been reliable all quarter, grew frustrated by the lack of accountability.

And Alex, always quick with a smirk, muttered, "Guess quotas are optional now."

Jason's credibility faltered—not because he didn't care, but because he confused kindness **with avoidance.**

Aha! Moment

Encouragement fuels growth, but accountability sustains it. When performance gaps persist, leadership requires both structure and fairness. A performance plan isn't punishment—it's a final opportunity for clarity, ownership, and restoration.

Maria's Coaching

Jason sat in Maria's office, frustration written across his face.

"I've coached Samantha, I've encouraged her, I've given her time," he said. "Nothing's changing. I don't want to be a nag."

Maria nodded slowly. "Jason, let me ask—what message do you think it sends to the team when someone misses expectations without consequence?"

Jason hesitated. "That standards don't really matter."

"And what message does it send to Samantha?" she pressed.

"That I don't believe she can meet them," he admitted quietly.

Maria leaned forward. "Exactly. Accountability isn't punishment — it's respect. It says, 'I believe you can meet this standard, and I'll give you structure to help you do it.' Encouragement alone isn't working because it lacks clarity. What would it look like if you added structure?"

Jason thought for a moment. "A performance plan."

Maria smiled. "Good. So what needs to be in it?"

Jason began listing ideas - metrics, timelines, support.

"Exactly," Maria said. "Accountability is more than clarity. It's structure, fairness, and follow-through. The goal isn't control, it's credibility–with her, and with your whole team."

Jason nodded. "Then I need a framework–something I can rely on when coaching isn't enough."

Maria smiled. "Try this: PERFORM. Diagnose the gap, Define expectations, Design achievable goals, Drive structure through timelines, Defend fairness with documentation, Discuss progress, and Demonstrate consistency. That's how you turn accountability into respect."

The PERFORM Framework

Performance Improvement Plans (PIPs) are often misunderstood as disciplinary measures. In reality, they're structured coaching tools—designed to give employees a fair, focused path to improvement.

The PERFORM Framework guides managers through that process—balancing accountability and empathy, precision and fairness. Each step builds upon the last: Diagnose, Define, Design, Drive, Defend, Discuss, and Demonstrate.

Pinpoint the Misses (Diagnose)

Start with clarity, not criticism. The first step in improving performance is identifying the exact gaps using objective data and observable behavior. Facts build fairness and keep the tone professional, allowing the conversation to focus on performance—not personality.

Sometimes, leaders rely on vague feedback ("You're not performing well"), speak from frustration instead of evidence, or focus on effort rather than measurable outcomes. Specificity turns emotion into evidence and sets the foundation for progress.

You can pinpoint effectively by

- Stating, "Quota was missed three months in a row at 72%, 68%, and 61%."
- Noting, "Follow-ups averaged 48 hours instead of the 24-hour team standard."
- Outlining, "Two client proposals were delayed beyond agreed timelines."

Diagnosis starts the healing. Keep it factual so accountability feels objective, not personal.

Establish Clear Expectations (Define)

Accountability only works when expectations are unmistakable. Define what success looks like in visible, measurable terms so there's no confusion between "trying" and "meeting expectations."

Leaders sometimes leave goals too broad, shift targets mid-plan, or assume the rep already knows what "good" means. Ambiguity breeds anxiety and avoidance. Clarity builds fairness and motivation.

You can define clearly by

- Setting, "Achieve $80K in new revenue this month."
- Requiring, "Submit pre-call plans before every client meeting."
- Reinforcing, "Attend all scheduled meetings on time."

Ambiguity breeds avoidance. Clarity creates fairness, and fairness drives motivation.

Realistic Goals (Design)

Design goals that stretch capability without breaking confidence. Realistic goals push performance forward but remain attainable within market conditions, skill level, and workload.

When leaders set goals that are impossible—or so easy they don't drive change—they lose credibility. Realism balances accountability with empathy, showing that the company wants improvement, not burnout.

You can design balanced goals by

- Doubling qualified meetings from four to eight per week.
- Shortening follow-up turnaround from 48 hours to 24.
- Raising proposal conversion rates by 10% within 45 days.

Realism earns trust. Goals should stretch performance, not credibility.

Frame the Timeline (Drive)

A strong plan needs a clock. Frame the total duration—typically 30, 60, or 90 days—and build in weekly check-ins to keep progress visible and energy consistent. Accountability thrives in rhythm, not randomness.

Many PIPs fail because managers leave plans open-ended ("We'll see how it goes"), skip midpoints, or review only at the end. Without structure, momentum fades.

You can maintain rhythm by

- Holding weekly review meetings every Friday at 3 PM.

- Scheduling a midpoint progress check with HR.
- Defining a "success by" date at plan conclusion.

Structure prevents drift. A plan without rhythm becomes wishful thinking.

Outline Documentation (Defend)

Documentation is protection—for the employee, the manager, and the company. Defend fairness by ensuring everything is written, shared, and transparent. Documentation clarifies expectations, progress, and outcomes for all parties.

Leaders weaken credibility when they rely on verbal updates, fail to involve HR, or keep inconsistent notes. Written alignment prevents misunderstandings and reinforces fairness.

You can document clearly by

- Using a written PIP signed by all parties.
- Maintaining a shared tracker logging actions and updates.
- Sending written summaries of each weekly review.

If it's not written, it's not real. Documentation protects both the rep and the company.

Review Progress (Discuss)

A plan is a conversation, not a document. Discuss progress weekly to reinforce ownership, recognize small wins, and address new challenges as they surface. Active dialogue turns formality into forward motion.

Some leaders avoid mid-plan discussions, focus only on final results, or overlook incremental progress. Those gaps make coaching feel mechanical instead of meaningful.

You can keep the dialogue alive by

- Reviewing metrics every Friday and celebrating visible improvement.
- Adjusting goals when new data or barriers emerge.
- Sharing positive client feedback to build momentum.

Silence kills accountability. Regular discussion keeps the plan alive.

Maintain Fairness (Demonstrate)

The final step—and the one everyone remembers—is fairness. Demonstrate consistency by applying the same standards, structure, and support across all reps. A fair process protects the employee's dignity and the leader's credibility.

PIPs lose their power when leaders show favoritism, treat the plan as punishment, or withdraw coaching support. Fairness turns what could feel punitive into a demonstration of leadership integrity.

You can model fairness by

- Using the same PIP process for similar performance gaps.
- Offering equal access to coaching, resources, and support.
- Measuring results through data, not personal bias.

Fairness is credibility. The team sees how you lead when things are hardest—that's when trust is built or broken.

> ### Research Spotlight: Why Performance Plans Matter
>
> *Gallup* (2019) found that only 14% of employees strongly agree their performance reviews inspire improvement. Structured plans close that gap by creating clarity and fairness.
>
> *SHRM (*2020) emphasizes that effective PIPs are developmental first and disciplinary second — restoring engagement through transparency and structure, not fear.

This time, Jason approached the situation differently. He gathered data on Samantha's performance, identifying where the gaps truly lay.

- Quotas missed at 72%, 68%, and 61%.
- Low client activity.
- Missed follow-ups.
- Lost deals from delayed responses.

He diagnosed the problem with clarity and evidence. (**Pinpoint the Misses**)

When they met, Jason stayed calm and direct.

"Samantha, here's where things stand. You've missed quota for three consecutive months, and I've documented gaps in client meetings, preparation, and follow-up. These issues are affecting both clients and our team's results. That's why we're moving to a structured performance plan."

He then defined success clearly.

"The plan's goal is to help you succeed, not to punish. You'll need to meet eight qualified client meetings per week, prepare pre-call plans before every meeting, and follow up with clients within 24 hours." (**Establish Clear Expectations**)

Next, he designed realistic, motivating goals.

"Your target for this month is $80K—achievable based on your current pipeline, but it'll require consistent execution. We'll track weekly progress together." (**Realistic Goals**)

He drove accountability through structure: a 60-day timeline, with weekly Friday reviews and a midpoint check-in with HR. Each milestone would show measurable progress. (**Frame the Timeline**)

Jason created a written PIP signed by both of them and co-signed by HR.

He included a shared progress tracker where Samantha could see updates in real time. (**Outline Documentation**)

Each week, Jason discussed progress openly. He reviewed the numbers, celebrated small wins, and provided feedback.

"You've doubled your meeting volume this week—that's great. Let's work next on tightening post-call notes." (**Review Progress**)

And through it all, Jason demonstrated fairness.

He held Samantha to the same structure he'd use for anyone else, staying objective, consistent, and supportive. (**Maintain Fairness**)

Over the next sixty days, Samantha showed renewed effort. Activity improved, preparation strengthened, and follow-ups became consistent. The outcome wasn't certain, but for the first time, the process was credible.

Accountability had shifted from confrontation to collaboration.

Chapter 12 Reflection Questions

RESPOND: What standards have you allowed to slip that may now require a formal plan?

_____

_____

_____

_____

REFLECT: Do you see performance plans as punishment or as a structured opportunity for growth and fairness?

_____

_____

_____

_____

REPEAT: How will you apply the PERFORM framework to make accountability consistent, credible, and fair across your team?

_____

_____

_____

_____

Hiring Right

"You don't hire for skills, you hire for attitude. Skills can always be taught."

Simon Sinek

Jason's team was finally finding its rhythm. Coaching was steady, accountability was taking hold, and performance was stabilizing.

But one issue remained—his old book of business.

For months, his team had covered Jason's accounts along with their own. It had worked temporarily, but cracks were forming. Deals slowed. Follow-ups lagged. Slack messages piled up about delays.

One afternoon, Maya pulled Jason aside. "We're doing our best," she said carefully, "but we're stretched too thin. When are we hiring your replacement?"

Jason knew she was right. Maria had already pressed him on it.

"Your team needs smaller, sharper books of business," she'd said. "You can't scale performance if people are overextended. It's time to hire."

Eager to prove he could handle it, Jason jumped in quickly. He wanted someone who could perform consistently and bring real talent to the team—someone experienced, driven, and capable of producing right away.

He zeroed in on résumés that looked strong: long tenure, President's Club awards, impressive logos. In the interview, the candidate spoke smoothly, hitting every talking point with confidence.

Jason convinced himself that past results equaled future reliability.

He hired fast.

At first, the numbers seemed fine—solid activity, decent pipeline.

But soon, deeper cracks appeared. The new hire pushed back on coaching, dismissed feedback, and spread negativity in subtle ways that eroded trust.

Instead of adding value, they created friction—questioning processes, undermining peers, and deflecting blame when deals slipped.

Unlike Alex's skeptical candor, this wasn't a healthy challenge—it was toxicity disguised as confidence.

Weeks later, after several coaching attempts, Jason realized the hire was a mistake. With Maria and HR's help, he made the hard call to let the rep go.

The team felt the disruption, and Jason felt the sting of rushing the process.

Aha! Moment

Filling a role isn't the same as hiring right. A bad hire doesn't just cost time—it drains culture, erodes trust, and slows everyone else's progress.

Maria's Coaching

Jason sighed. "He looked perfect on paper. Said all the right things. I thought he'd be great. What did I miss?"

Maria tilted her head. "Let me ask, what questions did you ask that revealed how he handled feedback?"

Jason thought for a moment. "None, really. I focused on performance—numbers, deals, experience."

"And how did he talk about his last team or manager?"

Jason frowned. "Now that I think about it, he blamed leadership for some things. I brushed it off."

Maria nodded. "That's the red flag. You weren't wrong to value performance. But great hires bring more than skill—they bring character, adaptability, and alignment. The résumé told you what he'd done. The interview should've told you who he is."

Jason nodded slowly. "So I should have been looking deeper—at how he learns, collaborates, and fits."

Maria smiled. "Exactly. That's what **TALENT** helps you see—Traits, Attitude, Learning Agility, Experience, Natural Fit, and Team Compatibility. You're not just hiring for today's results, but tomorrow's resilience."

Jason leaned back. "Then I need to slow down next time."

"Right," Maria said. "Hiring isn't about filling seats—it's about multiplying both performance and culture."

The TALENT Framework

Hiring right isn't about speed—it's about strength. The best leaders know that résumés reveal history, but TALENT reveals potential.

Great hires don't just perform—they elevate everyone around them. They show resilience under pressure, openness to feedback, and curiosity in how they grow. TALENT helps managers identify people who can both deliver results and strengthen culture.

When applied well, this framework transforms hiring from guesswork into a disciplined process that builds consistency, confidence, and long-term performance.

Traits

Traits are the foundation of long-term success—qualities like integrity, resilience, curiosity, humility, empathy, and discipline. They predict how someone will respond to pressure, change, and failure long before results do. Leaders who focus only on credentials often overlook the deeper signals that reveal character.

Hiring mistakes happen when managers prioritize polish over perseverance, charm over consistency, or credentials over character. True talent shows in how people handle adversity, not how well they interview.

You can identify strong traits by

- Asking, "Tell me about a time you failed and how you responded."
- Listening for curiosity in how they describe learning something new.
- Asking references for examples of dependability and follow-through.

Don't confuse polish with grit. Traits show in patterns, not performances.

Attitude

Attitude shapes how a person handles pressure, feedback, and collaboration. The right mindset—optimism, grit, and openness to coaching—determines whether someone grows or resists. While skills can be trained, attitude compounds.

Many leaders mistake enthusiasm for positivity, overlook subtle negativity, or ignore how candidates describe former colleagues. The way they talk about others often predicts how they'll show up in your culture.

You can uncover attitude by

- Asking, "What's the toughest feedback you've received, and what did you do about it?"
- Exploring, "How do you respond when something outside your control goes wrong?"
- Noting tone when they discuss past challenges or success.

Attitude compounds faster than skill. One person's outlook can lift—or corrode—an entire team.

Learning Agility

In a fast-changing environment, learning agility outweighs experience. Hire people who can absorb feedback, adapt quickly, and stay curious when things shift. Agility is the ability to learn, unlearn, and relearn faster than circumstances change.

Hiring mistakes occur when leaders equate tenure with adaptability, avoid real-time learning tests, or reward confidence over curiosity. True agility shows not in knowing everything, but in the willingness to learn anything.

You can evaluate agility by

- Running a short sales scenario to see how they adapt mid-conversation.
- Asking, "What's something you had to learn fast? How did you approach it?"
- Observing how they process feedback in the moment.

Agility isn't about knowing everything—it's about the willingness to learn anything.

Experience

Experience matters, but only when it validates growth and consistency. It confirms that skills were tested, refined, and applied—not just listed on paper. Great leaders use experience to complement judgment, not replace it.

Common missteps include overvaluing titles or awards, ignoring gaps in performance history, or assuming past success guarantees future fit. Experience should confirm capability, not carry the whole hire.

You can assess experience by

- Asking, "Walk me through your last two years of quota and what drove your results."
- Exploring, "What's one area you've improved most over your career?"
- Checking references for patterns, not just highlight stories.

Experience is evidence, not destiny. Growth matters more than glamour.

Natural Fit

Fit isn't sameness—it's alignment. The best hires share the organization's values but bring fresh perspective and complementary strengths. A true fit strengthens diversity of thought while reinforcing cultural consistency.

Leaders often hire people who mirror their own personality, equate fit with comfort, or ignore deeper motivators and values. Comfort may feel good in the short term but often limits innovation long term.

You can evaluate fit by

- Asking, "What kind of team environment helps you thrive?"
- Exploring, "What about our mission or culture excites you most?"
- Probing for alignment with company purpose and values.

Hire for complementarity, not comfort. Diversity fuels innovation.

Team Compatibility

No hire operates in isolation. Compatibility ensures collaboration, trust, and stability across relationships. The best hires fit not just the role—but the rhythm of the team.

Mistakes happen when leaders make decisions without peer input, ignore how candidates interact in groups, or overlook early signs of friction. A strong fit is built on mutual respect, not instant chemistry.

You can evaluate compatibility by

- Including a peer or partner from another department in the interview process.
- Observing whether the candidate listens as much as they speak.
- Asking the team afterward, "Would you want to work with them?"

Compatibility doesn't mean instant chemistry—it means mutual respect and the potential to collaborate productively.

Research Spotlight: Why Hiring Right Matters

The *U.S. Department of Labor* estimates that a bad hire costs up to 30% of first-year earnings.

Deloitte (2018) found that poor hiring decisions ripple through morale, productivity, and retention. Conversely, structured hiring—grounded in traits, agility, and fit—leads to faster ramp times and stronger performance consistency.

Leaders who slow down to assess TALENT beyond résumés consistently outperform those who hire on speed and surface-level skill.

This time, Jason slowed the process down. He built his questions around **TALENT**.

He began by asking, "Tell me about a time you faced repeated rejection. How did you respond?"

The candidate shared a thoughtful story of persistence and reflection. Jason noted the authenticity and self-awareness. (**Traits & Attitude**)

When discussing past teams, she spoke with humility and credit, not blame. It showed character.

Next, Jason ran a quick role-play. The candidate adapted mid-scenario, adjusting tone and questions naturally. She didn't need perfection—she showed coachability. (**Learning Agility**)

He then reviewed experience. "Walk me through your last two years of quota and what you learned from both wins and losses."

Her honesty impressed him. She knew her metrics and owned her growth. (**Experience**)

Finally, he invited Maya into the panel. Afterward, Jason asked her thoughts.

Maya smiled. "She listens first and asks sharp questions. That's a good fit for us." (**Team Compatibility**)

Please Note: Aligning TALENT with HR

Hiring frameworks like TALENT strengthen fairness and consistency, but they should work alongside HR, not replace it.

HR ensures compliance; TALENT ensures culture and capability.

Together, they create a balanced process that's structured, fair, and effective.

When the new hire joined, the difference was immediate. She leaned into feedback, collaborated with peers, and even asked to role-play tough calls her first week. Her performance grew quickly, and so did team morale.

Jason realized he hadn't just filled a seat; he'd multiplied capability. The right hire brought skill, humility, and strength—the combination that drives sustained performance.

But leadership isn't only about bringing in great people. Sometimes it means letting go when performance still doesn't improve, a lesson Jason was about to face next.

Chapter 13 Reflection Questions

RESPOND: What's one adjustment you'll make to my next interview using TALENT?

_____
_____
_____
_____

REFLECT: Which past hire taught you the most—and what signals did you miss or catch?

_____
_____
_____
_____

REPEAT: How can you make TALENT a consistent part of your process so every hire strengthens both culture and performance?

_____
_____
_____
_____

Leading Through Separation

"Culture isn't built by the people you hire. Culture's upheld by the standards you enforce."

Adapted from an Anonymous Quote

CHAPTER FOURTEEN

The Seller's Framework – From Seller to Sales

Jason dreaded the conversation. Samantha had now missed quota for five straight months—despite coaching, clear expectations, and a sixty-day performance improvement plan.

Still, he hesitated.

When she walked into their one-on-one, Jason forced a smile. "How are you feeling about this quarter?"

Samantha shrugged. "I know it hasn't been great, but I'm working on it."

Jason nodded quickly. "Yeah, I'm sure you'll bounce back. Let's just give it some more time."

He said the words, but even as he did, he knew they weren't true.

She wasn't turning it around. He told himself he was protecting her, but in reality, he was avoiding what came next.

The impact spread quietly.

Maya grew frustrated covering extra deals.

Jordan whispered, "Do standards even matter anymore?"

And Alex, always perceptive, muttered, "Guess some people are untouchable."

Jason's indecision wasn't protecting Samantha—it was hurting everyone.

Aha! Moment

Separation is one of the hardest responsibilities in leadership. But avoiding it for too long damages trust, morale, and performance far more than the act itself.

Maria's Coaching

Jason sank into the chair across from Maria's desk, eyes tired.

"I don't want to ruin her career," he said. "She's trying, she's a good person. I keep thinking if I just give her more time, she'll make it."

Maria tilted her head. "Let me ask—what does 'more time' change that the last five months didn't?"

Jason paused. "Probably nothing."

"And how's this delay affecting the rest of your team?"

Jason sighed. "They're frustrated. Maya's picking up extra deals. Alex thinks I'm playing favorites. Even Jordan's starting to question things."

Maria nodded slowly. "So who are you really protecting?"

Jason rubbed his temples. "I guess...no one. Not her, not the team."

Maria leaned forward, tone calm but firm. "You've already given her structure, feedback, and time. Accountability isn't cruelty, Jason—it's clarity and respect. The moment you avoid the standard, you confuse the whole team."

Jason nodded quietly.

Maria continued, "So the goal now isn't to end it perfectly—it's to do it right. With care, fairness, and professionalism. That's what **ACT** is for: **Align expectations, Communicate clearly, and Transition the team**. You don't rush it. You prepare, and you protect everyone involved."

Jason exhaled, already replaying the steps in his mind. "So it's not about being heartless."

Maria smiled. "No. It's about being honest."

The ACT Framework

Separating from a team member is never easy, but it's one of the defining tests of leadership. Avoiding it undermines fairness, damages morale, and erodes credibility.

The ACT Framework gives leaders a structured way to approach separation with clarity, fairness, and respect—ensuring the process is handled both professionally and compassionately.

Each step protects three things: the individual's dignity, the team's trust, and the leader's credibility.

Align Expectations

Before any separation occurs, alignment must come first. Every expectation, coaching step, and performance plan should be clearly documented and communicated. This ensures the employee understands where they stand and eliminates surprises that damage trust.

When eaders move forward without HR alignment, skip proper documentation, or avoid clear conversations early in the process-separation feels abrupt and unfair.

You can align expectations effectively by

- Stating, "We outlined expectations for client meetings and quota in your PIP."
- Reminding, "The action plan called for three weekly updates—here's what's been missed."
- Confirming, "We've reviewed progress together weekly, and the gaps have remained consistent."

Documentation protects both the employee and the leader. Partner early with HR to confirm that all prior steps and communications are complete and consistent.

Communicate Clearly

When it's time to deliver the decision, clarity and empathy must work together. Communicate the outcome directly, respectfully, and without unnecessary explanation or debate. The goal is to preserve dignity while ensuring the message is unmistakable.

Avoid overexplaining, growing defensive, or delegating the conversation entirely to HR. Others use cold or distant language that strips away respect. The best leaders stay calm, factual, and human.

You can communicate clearly by

- Saying, "We've reviewed your performance over several months, and the expectations have not been met. Today will be your last day with the company."
- Adding, "We appreciate your efforts and wish you success as you move forward."
- Acknowledging, "I know this is difficult, but I want you to hear this directly and respectfully."

Clarity and tone matter equally. Your words deliver closure; your demeanor delivers respect.

Transition the Team

Once the separation is complete, leadership focus must shift from the individual to the team. How you handle the aftermath determines whether trust and morale strengthen or fracture. Communicate with professionalism, protect confidentiality, and restore focus quickly.

Leaders often mishandle this step—either oversharing private details, avoiding the topic entirely, or lingering too long on the loss. The goal isn't to justify the decision, but to reinforce stability and direction.

You can transition the team effectively by

- Announcing, "Samantha is no longer with the company. We're grateful for her contributions and will continue moving forward together."
- Reassuring, "If anyone has concerns about their own performance, my door is open."

- Refocusing, "We're redistributing accounts to balance workloads and keep momentum strong."

Transition isn't just what you say—it's how you lead afterward. Your tone sets the emotional direction for the team.

> ### Research Spotlight: Why Separation Done Well Matters
> Avoiding separation with disengaged or underperforming employees can reduce team productivity.
>
> *Gallup* (2019) showed that teams lose morale and trust when standards aren't upheld. When handled correctly, respectful separations strengthen leadership credibility and rebuild cultural trust faster than avoidance ever can.

Jason didn't delay this time. He reviewed Samantha's missed quotas, documented coaching notes, and her formal PIP progress. He aligned every detail with HR and Maria to ensure fairness and compliance. (**Align Expectations**)

On the morning of the meeting, Jason rehearsed his words—not to make them sound perfect, but to ensure they came out steady and respectful.

He and HR met with Samantha together. Jason's voice was calm.

"Samantha, over the past several months, we've worked through coaching plans and a formal improvement plan. Unfortunately, the expectations we outlined haven't been met. Because of that, today will be your last day with the company."

He paused to let it land.

"I know this is difficult. You've contributed meaningfully to this team, and we appreciate your efforts. We truly wish you the best in what comes next." (**Communicate Clearly**)

Samantha nodded, eyes glossy but calm.

"I understand," she said quietly. "Thank you for being honest."

> ### Sidebar: Partner with HR, Don't Go It Alone
>
> Involve HR early, not only when termination is near. HR provides structure, ensures compliance, and acts as a neutral partner to guide documentation, communication, and timing.
>
> If a PIP becomes necessary, HR should co-author it with you to ensure fairness and legal protection. And when separation becomes unavoidable, HR's involvement ensures clarity, professionalism, and compassion for all parties. Partnership with HR doesn't remove leadership responsibility, it reinforces it.

After the conversation, Jason met with the team. His tone was professional but human.

"I want to let you know that Samantha is no longer with the company. We're grateful for her contributions, and I want you to know this decision was made after every effort to support improvement. We'll move forward together and keep our focus on what's next." (**Transition the Team**)

The room was quiet at first. Maya exhaled, Jordan nodded thoughtfully, and even Alex sat still, saying nothing.

There was a shared understanding—not of celebration, but of clarity. The uncertainty had ended. The standard was visible again.

Jason hadn't enjoyed the process, but he'd led it with integrity. The separation had been painful, but it had also restored credibility—both to his leadership and to the team's trust in their direction.

And though the team was steady again, Maria reminded him later, "Clarity isn't just for when things end. It's also how you prevent these moments from repeating."

That truth would shape Jason's next focus: creating the kind of environment where strong performance and accountability could grow together.

Chapter 14 Reflection Questions

RESPOND: What expectations have you clearly aligned and documented with struggling reps?

_____

_____

_____

_____

REFLECT: Where might you be avoiding a hard conversation the team already feels?

_____

_____

_____

_____

REPEAT: How will you use ACT to ensure separation is handled with clarity, fairness, and care?

_____

_____

_____

_____

Turning Critics into Allies

"If everyone is thinking alike, then somebody isn't thinking."

George S. Patton

CHAPTER FIFTEEN

Jason's team had finally found its rhythm.

Jordan had grown more confident, Maya remained steady, and the new hire Jason had brought on months ago had fully integrated—curious, coachable, and quick to collaborate.

The group functioned well together. Almost. Alex still pushed back.

He wasn't disruptive, but his sharp, skeptical nature surfaced often. When something didn't seem practical, he said so. When a plan felt rushed, he challenged it. His questions were rarely unfounded, but his tone could stall momentum—and everyone looked to Jason for how to respond.

In one meeting, Jason laid out an initiative to improve conversion rates by tightening late-stage deal reviews.

Before he finished, Alex jumped in.

"We've tried this before," he said. "Last time it slowed deals down instead of speeding them up."

Jason felt the tension build. He had little time and a forecast meeting in an hour.

"Alex," he snapped, "that's not helpful. Let's move on."

The room went quiet. Alex leaned back, crossing his arms.

Maya glanced down, the new hire froze, and Jason realized in seconds—he hadn't just silenced Alex, he'd silenced everyone.

Aha! Moment

Critics aren't enemies. They can either sharpen your strategy or stall your progress—depending on how you handle them.

Maria's Coaching

Jason dropped into Maria's office later that day. "I've done everything I can with Alex, and he still challenges everything. I'm losing patience."

Maria tilted her head. "Why do you think he challenges so often?"

Jason shrugged. "Because he likes being difficult."

Maria smiled slightly. "Maybe. Or maybe he cares. If he didn't, he'd stay quiet."

Jason frowned. "So caring looks like constant pushback?"

"Sometimes," Maria said. "Critics are often the ones who see risks early. The problem isn't that they speak up, it's how we respond when they do. What did you teach the team today?"

Jason sighed. "That dissent isn't safe."

Maria nodded. "So, the question isn't how to stop Alex from speaking up, it's how to guide the conversation so it helps instead of hinders. Try ALLY: Acknowledge, Listen, Link, and Yes-or-No with Why. It gives you a way to use dissent productively instead of fighting it."

Jason leaned forward. "So I don't have to agree with him, but I can still learn from him."

"Exactly," Maria said. "Critics who care can become your strongest allies if you handle them with structure."

The ALLY Framework

Critics and dissenters can be a leader's best reality check—or their biggest frustration. The difference lies in structure. Without it, leaders either silence dissent (losing valuable insight) or let it dominate (losing focus).

The ALLY Framework helps leaders channel dissent productively: welcome the voice, examine the merit, connect the value, and close the loop clearly. When practiced consistently, it transforms tension into trust and sharpens the quality of collective decision-making.

Acknowledge

The first step is to make critique safe. When team members speak up, they're taking a risk—testing whether honesty is rewarded or punished. Acknowledgment signals that feedback and challenge are not only permitted but valued. It doesn't mean agreement; it means respect for the courage to contribute.

Leaders often make the mistake of dismissing input because of timing or tone, reacting defensively, or showing appreciation only for agreement. Over time, this trains teams to stay silent. Acknowledging input neutrally—without judgment—keeps dialogue open and builds psychological safety.

You might say

- "That's a good concern to raise—thanks for surfacing it."
- "I hear what you're saying. Let's explore it briefly."
- "I appreciate you speaking up, even if we see it differently."

Acknowledge without agreeing. Respect the courage to speak, not necessarily the content of the critique.

Listen

After acknowledgment comes listening—real, focused listening that seeks to understand, not to respond. Leaders who jump in too quickly to defend their position send the message that challenges are futile. Listening fully allows insight to surface and helps separate emotion from information.

At the same time, listening without structure can lead to derailment or debate. Letting one critique dominate the meeting or accepting unverified claims can muddy progress. The goal is to ask clarifying questions that transform opinion into context and help everyone focus on the facts.

Try prompts like

- "Can you share an example of when that happened?"
- "What risk are you seeing that we might be missing?"
- "Help me understand what outcome you're worried about."

Listen deeply but keep it focused. The goal is to understand, not to debate endlessly.

Link

Listening without action leads to frustration. Once the concern is understood, decide whether it holds value—and, if so, link it to a clear next step. This demonstrates that input matters and creates a bridge between discussion and improvement.

Leaders can fall into two traps: acknowledging feedback but never acting on it, or overhauling plans entirely in response to one perspective. Linking keeps balance. It integrates useful insight while keeping the broader goal intact.

For example

- "That's helpful feedback—let's add a checkpoint before rollout."
- "Good point. We'll clarify that step to avoid confusion."
- "Let's note this as a learning we incorporate in future campaigns."

Use what's useful without losing focus. Integrate value selectively and move forward.

Yes / No & Why

Every discussion needs closure. Whether you adopt the suggestion, test it, or move on, closing the loop ensures transparency and fairness. Explaining the "why" behind your decision—especially when saying no—prevents resentment and reinforces trust.

Be careful to avoid closure to spare feelings or end discussions abruptly without rationale. Both approaches leave people uncertain or unheard. Clear reasoning communicates respect even in disagreement and helps others see how decisions align with priorities and data.

You could respond

- "Yes—we'll include that adjustment; it strengthens the plan."
- "No—we'll keep our current approach because the data shows it's working."
- "We'll pilot your idea on a small scale before wider rollout."

Always explain your decision. Transparency earns more respect than silent dismissal.

Research Spotlight: The Value of Constructive Dissent

Harvard Business Review (2016) found that teams with constructive dissent outperform teams with artificial harmony.

Google's Project *Aristotle* identified psychological safety as the top predictor of team performance. When dissent is welcomed, guided, and closed with clarity, teams innovate faster and align stronger.

At the next meeting, Jason handled things differently.

When Alex voiced another concern about a proposed client engagement plan, Jason paused.

"Thanks for raising that, Alex. What risk are you seeing?" **(Acknowledge, Listen)**

Alex explained his perspective, outlining where similar projects had stalled due to misaligned expectations.

Jason nodded. "Good callout. Let's build in a clearer milestone review at the midpoint so we don't repeat that." **(Link)**

He continued, "We'll add that checkpoint, but we're keeping the rest of the approach—it's still the best fit for our timeline." (**Yes / No & Why**)

The tone shifted immediately. Alex leaned forward, engaged rather than combative.

The rest of the team saw that feedback didn't need to be feared or ignored—it could refine the plan without derailing progress.

From that meeting on, discussions grew sharper, faster, and more balanced.

Jason didn't turn Alex into a cheerleader, but he turned him into an ally—someone who challenged ideas without challenging leadership.

He realized that real influence doesn't silence critics. It channels them.

Chapter 15 Reflection Questions

RESPOND: Who on your team, or in your organization, often challenges your ideas? How can you apply ALLY to draw value from their perspective?

_____
_____
_____
_____

REFLECT: Do you tend to shut down dissent too quickly or let it go too far before redirecting?

_____
_____
_____
_____

REPEAT: How can you model healthy dissent until your team learns to challenge ideas without challenging alignment?

_____
_____
_____
_____

Sustaining Leadership

"Becoming a leader is synonymous with becoming yourself. It is that simple, and it is precisely that difficult."

Warren Bennis

Jason found himself once again in the same conference room where, nearly a year earlier, Maria had first told him he was ready to lead.

The notebook in front of him looked similar—scribbles, plans, reflections—but the man holding the pen was different.

He had survived the whirlwind of his first year: hiring mistakes, performance plans, tough separations, breakthroughs in coaching, and the challenge of turning skeptics into contributors. His team was performing well, trust was high, and they had exceeded quota for the quarter.

And yet, beneath the success, Jason felt a quiet unease.

He'd built structure and stability, but lately, growth had slowed. Meetings felt repetitive. Coaching sessions felt mechanical. He was managing the work, but not growing as a leader.

Aha! Moment

Year one builds structure. Year two tests whether you can sustain it. The moment you stop growing, your leadership starts coasting.

Maria's Coaching

Maria smiled as she walked in. "One year of leadership under your belt. How's it feel?"

Jason laughed softly. "Honestly? Good, and a little flat. I've hit a groove, but I think I've slipped into comfort. My coaching's steady, but I'm not learning like I used to. Between meetings, forecasts, and one-on-ones, I've stopped feeding myself."

Maria nodded. "That's more common than you think. Most new leaders spend their second year reacting—meetings, reports, the urgent replacing the important. They stop investing in their own growth, and their team follows suit."

Jason frowned. "So it's not just me?"

"Not at all," Maria said. "The danger of leadership isn't failure, it's drift. You build systems like ORDER, PLAN, CONSIST, and REAL to stabilize performance. But sustaining them takes renewal, reflection, and the humility to keep learning. The next stage of leadership isn't about surviving—it's about learning to **THRIVE**."

The THRIVE Framework

Leadership isn't a milestone; it's a marathon. Sustained leaders don't just manage performance—they maintain energy, adaptability, and purpose long after the first year's urgency fades.

The THRIVE Framework reinforces everything you've learned: structure from ORDER, planning from PLAN, consistency from CONSIST, and accountability from REAL—while adding the missing piece: long-term renewal. This framework equips leaders to sustain momentum, balance ambition with endurance, and continue growing themselves while guiding others.

Targets & Tracking

Growth isn't static—it's a moving target. Many leaders set ambitious goals early in the year, only to let them fade amid shifting priorities. Others cling to outdated metrics that no longer reflect the business reality. Sustained leadership means revisiting and refining goals regularly, ensuring that progress is measured by both performance and development.

Strong leaders track two things: what gets done and how it gets done. They build checkpoints into the year, align evolving priorities with organizational goals, and keep motivation alive by connecting outcomes to purpose.

Examples

- Reassessing goals each quarter to reflect new business realities.
- Tracking both "what" (quota) and "how" (skill development).
- Adjusting metrics as the team's maturity evolves.

Goals should stretch but not scatter. Too many create confusion; too few create complacency.

Habits & Rhythms

Leadership is sustained through rhythm. The cadence of meetings, one-on-ones, and reflection sessions forms the heartbeat of the team. When those habits fade, so does connection and accountability. Many leaders cancel one-on-ones when things get busy or let team huddles drift into routine status reports instead of performance-driving conversations.

Great leaders refresh their rhythms before they go stale. They evolve meeting structures to fit the team's growth, vary voices to maintain engagement, and ensure every recurring touchpoint has a clear purpose. Rhythm creates trust; intentional refresh keeps it meaningful.

Examples

- Protecting one-on-ones as non-negotiable touchpoints.
- Refreshing meeting agendas every quarter to maintain focus.
- Introducing rotating voices or themes to keep energy high.

Rhythms provide structure, but don't mistake structure for progress. Revisit purpose regularly so routines don't become ruts.

Renewal & Rest

Burnout, not inexperience, is the top reason leaders plateau. Many equate long hours with dedication, but exhaustion erodes clarity, patience, and decision-making. Renewal is the act of recharging so you can lead with steadiness instead of strain.

The most sustainable leaders protect their energy like any other asset. They model balance for their teams, demonstrate boundaries without guilt, and normalize recovery as part of high performance. Renewal doesn't weaken leadership—it sustains it.

Examples

- Blocking regular "recovery" days after major projects.
- Modeling healthy boundaries—logging off on time, taking breaks.
- Encouraging your team to do the same without guilt.

Renewal isn't retreat; it's readiness. You can't pour from an empty tank.

Input & Insight

Leaders who stop learning stop leading. Tenure never replaces curiosity. Complacency often creeps in quietly—when leaders assume what worked last year still applies or stop seeking feedback because "the system works."

Ongoing growth requires active learning. The best leaders continually seek outside perspectives, welcome feedback, and challenge their own assumptions. They stay curious long after they become competent, turning feedback into evolution rather than defense.

Examples
- Asking peers for feedback on communication or strategy.
- Attending a leadership workshop each quarter.
- Reviewing recorded calls or meetings for self-assessment.

Seek input with filters. Welcome new ideas but align them with your team's mission and maturity.

Value in Others

Your leadership only scales when others grow. Many managers fall into the trap of hoarding critical responsibilities, focusing only on outcomes, or investing solely in top performers. Sustainable leaders know that progress multiplies when everyone develops.

Valuing others means consistently mentoring, delegating, and recognizing growth. It's about helping your people build confidence through challenge, not comfort. Growth isn't an event—it's a rhythm of recognition and stretch.

Examples

- Assigning stretch projects to emerging talent.
- Recognizing effort, not just results, in public forums.
- Building development goals into every performance plan.

Don't just develop the willing; invest in the potential. Consistent investment creates consistent performance.

Evolve

Markets shift. Teams mature. Priorities change. Yet many leaders cling to what worked before, either out of comfort or fear of change. Others overcorrect, chasing every new idea or tool without discernment. Maturity in leadership means adapting with purpose—anchored in principle, but flexible in practice.

To evolve is to grow intentionally. It's recognizing when old playbooks no longer serve and experimenting with new approaches to stay relevant. The best leaders evolve before they're forced to, modeling adaptability that keeps teams confident through change.

Examples

- Adjusting your coaching style as your team gains experience.
- Experimenting with new technologies that enhance efficiency.
- Testing new communication rhythms for hybrid or remote teams.

Evolve with purpose. Adapt methods, not values.

> ### Research Spotlight: Sustaining Growth Over Time
>
> A 2021 *Deloitte* study found that 77% of professionals experience recurring burnout, but the root cause isn't always workload. It's lack of renewal and clarity. Leaders who intentionally schedule recovery, reflection, and recalibration report 55% higher engagement and 40% greater retention in their teams.
>
> Sustained leadership comes from disciplined balance—structure, rest, and curiosity in equal measure.

Later that afternoon, Jason stayed behind in the office, notebook open.

This time, his reflection wasn't about what he'd done wrong; it was about how to keep getting better.

He began by revisiting his goals. He wrote three categories at the top of the page: *Team Performance, Personal Growth,* and *People Development.* (**Targets & Tracking**)

He broke down what had worked and what had drifted. One-on-ones? Consistent, but repetitive. Team meetings? Productive, but predictable. Coaching? Steady, but lacking creativity. (**Habits & Rhythms**)

He flipped to a clean page and wrote one word at the top: *Renewal.* He circled it twice.

The last few months had been relentless—forecast reviews, hiring decisions, back-to-back meetings. He realized he hadn't taken a real break in months. (**Renewal & Rest**)

Jason blocked time for recovery, both for himself and his team. Then he wrote: *Find new input.* He added reminders to schedule peer shadow sessions and leadership roundtables with other managers. (**Input & Insight**)

He smiled as he wrote the next line: *Develop someone to eventually replace me.*

It wasn't ego—it was the measure of true leadership. He listed names of reps ready for stretch projects. (**Value in Others**)

Finally, in bold letters, he wrote: *Evolve.*

Next to it, he added: "Keep learning, keep adapting, stay hungry." (**Evolve**)

He closed the notebook, realizing that sustainability wasn't about perfection—it was about discipline, renewal, and humility.

Leadership wasn't a promotion to protect; it was a muscle to keep building.

Chapter 16 Reflection Questions

RESPOND: How will you protect your energy and balance to lead well long-term?

_____

_____

_____

_____

REFLECT: Where do you risk slipping into comfort or plateauing?

_____

_____

_____

_____

REPEAT: What rhythms and learning habits will you reinforce week after week to keep growing as a leader?

_____

_____

_____

_____

Conclusion

*"Knowledge is not power.
Applied knowledge is."*

Dale Carnegie

Jason closed his office door and let the quiet settle.

The quarter was over, the numbers were in, and the team had grown stronger—not just in results, but in trust, rhythm, and resilience.

Looking back, he realized the biggest lessons hadn't come from hitting quota.

They came from the difficult moments—the hard conversations, the accountability plans, the hiring decisions, and the self-doubt that forced him to grow.

Success looked different now.

It wasn't defined by his personal pipeline, but by Jordan's growing confidence, Alex's sharpened contributions, and a new rep who had strengthened the team's culture from day one.

Leadership, he realized, wasn't about his individual wins. It was about multiplying others.

That evening, Jason drove home to the house he and his wife had bought just months earlier—a milestone that once felt out of reach.

His wife was packing for their upcoming vacation, a reminder of how far they had come since the early years of uncertainty.

Jason smiled, realizing that success wasn't just professional anymore.

It was deeply personal—the quiet balance between the life he was building and the people he cared about most.

He thought back to where it began. As a rep, he learned how to prepare, open, and discover—*The Fundamentals of Selling*. Later, he stretched into executive meetings, procurement battles, and stakeholder alignment—*Winning Complex Sales*. And now, he had crossed into the hardest and most rewarding stage of all—*From Seller to Sales Leader*, where the focus shifted from hitting numbers to developing people.

Every stage had stretched him.
- Every framework had anchored him.
- And every mistake had shaped him into the leader he was becoming.

Maria's voice echoed in his mind, steady and familiar: *"Sales isn't just about numbers. It's about building the life you want."*

Jason smiled, understanding now that leadership was no different. It wasn't about titles, quotas, or finish lines. It was about responsibility, growth, and the people you choose to multiply along the way.

For the Reader

The same is true for you.

Finishing this book isn't the finish line—it's your starting line. Retention doesn't come from reading once. It comes from application, practice, and reflection.

- Apply what you've learned.
- Revisit the frameworks.

- Use them in real conversations—with your team, your peers, and yourself.

Each time you return, the lessons will meet you at a new stage of your journey—because your perspective will have grown.

Build habits that turn knowledge into skill.

Reflect often. Coach others. And never stop practicing.

Aha! Moment
Growth isn't about what you know.
It's about what you consistently practice.

Looking Ahead

Jason's story isn't finished, and neither is yours.

From his first shaky discovery calls, to navigating executive boardrooms, to leading through coaching, accountability, and even separation, his journey mirrors the growth every sales professional eventually faces.

The Seller's Framework series will continue, diving deeper into each framework introduced so far. Future books will expand these concepts, not as quick guides, but as field-ready resources designed to help you practice, teach, and lead through them.

Each will explore a specific skill set—how to prepare, align, coach, influence, and sustain results across any environment. Alongside the books, new tools and training resources will help you apply these lessons in your own world, one framework at a time.

So, pause for a moment and ask yourself:

- What are you building?
- Who are you multiplying?
- What does success truly look like—for your career, your family, your life?

Keep learning. Keep growing. Keep building. The journey continues.

Enjoy the Book?

Thank you for reading *From Seller to Sales Leader*. If you enjoyed the book, would you mind leaving a review on Amazon? It provides the opportunity for others to benefit, & helps me to provide further books on sales & leadership.

Thank you!

https://www.amazon.com/review/create-review/?ie=UTF8&channel=glance-detail&asin=B0G66ZBC87

Provide Amazon review for
From Seller to Sales Leader

Reader Toolkit
& Appendix

Use this toolkit as your daily and weekly leadership checklist. For each situation—whether you're coaching, forecasting, hiring, or handling accountability—mark which frameworks you've practiced and where you still need to grow. The more consistently you apply these, the more instinctive your leadership becomes.

LEADER — Foundations of Leadership

- **Lead Self**: Manage your time, energy, and focus before leading others.
- **Engage Others**: Listen deeply, build trust, and connect through presence.
- **Adapt with Flexibility**: Adjust your style while maintaining standards.
- **Develop People**: Coach for growth, not dependence.
- **Empower Others**: Delegate ownership and celebrate initiative.
- **Reflect & Refine**: Evaluate regularly and turn lessons into habits.

COACH — Coaching in Action

- **Clarify the Situation**: Start by defining the issue or goal clearly. Focus on facts, patterns, and desired outcomes before jumping to solutions.
- **Offer Space and Observe**: Pause to understand the rep's mindset. Notice tone, body language, and ownership level before responding.
- **Ask Powerful Questions**: Guide reflection through curiosity — questions that uncover insight, not defensiveness.

- **Confirm Understanding**: Restate what you've heard to ensure alignment and demonstrate active listening.
- **Help Expand Perspective**: Challenge assumptions, surface new options, and encourage commitment to action.

INSPECT — Pipeline & Forecast Discipline

- **Inputs**: Keep CRM data clean, current, and accurate.
- **Numbers**: Track coverage ratios, conversion rates, and trends.
- **Signals**: Look for verifiable buying intent, not verbal optimism.
- **Progress**: Monitor deal movement and address stalls early.
- **Evidence**: Require proof at each stage before advancing.
- **Commit**: Forecast based on proof, not hope.
- **Time**: Maintain a weekly inspection cadence and stay consistent.

PLAN — Structuring Leadership

- **Priorities**: Protect time for what's truly important, not just urgent.
- **Lean on Others**: Delegate ownership to grow confidence and capability.
- **Agenda**: Bring clarity and direction to every meeting.
- **Next Steps**: Always close conversations with clear owners and timelines.

BRIDGE — Balancing Up and Down

- **Brief the Why**: Explain both the company's goals and what's in it for the team.

- **Reflect Concerns**: Acknowledge emotions and frustrations before problem-solving.
- **Involve Key Voices**: Invite input from influencers and skeptics early.
- **Define the Message**: Translate leadership's direction into clear, actionable language your team understands and can execute.
- **Ground in Evidence**: Support communication with data, results, or stories that build credibility and answer "why now."
- **Escalate Upward**: Share balanced, evidence-backed feedback with leadership.

CONSIST — Coaching Rhythm

- **Cadence**: Protect weekly one-on-ones as non-negotiable.
- **Observe**: Ground feedback in real calls and behavior, not assumptions.
- **Notes & Preparation**: Come prepared; expect reps to do the same.
- **Shared Ownership**: Make reps responsible for their growth.
- **Informal Access**: Be available for real-time coaching moments.
- **Small Wins**: Recognize incremental improvements often.
- **Track Progress**: Document and review growth over time.

CLEAR — Accountability Conversations

- **Clarify** the Situation: Identify the performance gap or missed expectation with facts, not emotion.

- **Listen to Understand**: Hear the rep's perspective without interrupting or judging. Understanding the "why" behind behavior builds credibility.
- **Examine Root Causes**: Go beyond surface excuses to uncover what's really driving the gap—skills, effort, clarity, or mindset.
- **Align on Solutions**: Collaboratively define what success looks like, setting specific, measurable next steps and ownership.
- **Reinforce Commitment**: Summarize agreements, set follow-ups, and hold both sides accountable for action.

LINK — Cross-Department Collaboration

- **Listen First**: Seek to understand other departments' goals and pressures.
- **Identify Shared Goals**: Find the overlap between their success and yours.
- **Navigate Differences**: Address conflict with empathy and business focus.
- **Keep Aligned**: Maintain rhythm and transparency through shared updates.

PERFORM — Performance Plans

- **Pinpoint the Misses**: Use data to name specific performance gaps.
- **Establish Clear Expectations**: Define measurable standards for success.
- **Realistic Goals**: Create achievable steps that restore confidence.
- **Frame the Timeline**: Set specific 30/60/90-day checkpoints.

- **Outline Documentation**: Keep the process transparent and fair.
- **Review Progress**: Evaluate regularly, not just at the end.
- **Maintain Fairness**: Apply the same structure to everyone equally.

ACT — Leading Through Separation

- **Align Expectations**: Ensure clarity and documentation before action.
- **Communicate Clearly**: Be factual, concise, and compassionate.
- **Transition the Team**: Maintain trust and professionalism post-separation.

TALENT — Hiring Right

- **Traits**: Integrity, curiosity, resilience—qualities that outlast skill.
- **Attitude**: Optimism, humility, and openness to feedback.
- **Learning** Agility: Ability to learn fast and adapt.
- **Experience**: Relevant, consistent performance—without ego.
- **Natural Fit**: Alignment with values and culture.
- **Team Compatibility**: Collaboration and respect within team dynamics.

ALLY — Turning Critics into Allies

- **Acknowledge:** Recognize their perspective and thank them for speaking up.
- **Listen:** Understand their reasoning without defensiveness.

- **Leverage:** Extract the useful insight to strengthen the plan.
- **Yes / No & Why:** Close the loop with a clear decision and rationale—adopt the idea (and credit it) or explain why you aren't using it so the team sees the logic.

THRIVE — Sustaining Leadership Growth

- **Targets & Tracking**: Revisit goals often and adapt to change.
- **Habits & Rhythms**: Maintain structure and consistency.
- **Renewal & Rest**: Protect your energy and clarity.
- **Input & Insight**: Keep learning and seeking perspective.
- **Value in Others**: Develop, empower, and multiply your team.
- **Evolve**: Stay adaptable as challenges and markets change.

Daily Leadership Reminders

- Coach every week.
- Inspect what you expect.
- Protect priorities, not just schedule.
- Address issues early—with care and clarity.
- Celebrate small wins, sustain big rhythms.
- Grow yourself as deliberately as you grow your team.

Reference
& Research Guide

The Seller's Framework – From Seller to Sales

Leadership & Management

- Bennis, W. (1989). On Becoming a Leader. Basic Books.
- Center for Creative Leadership. (2019). "Leadership Transitions: The Challenges New Leaders Face." CCL Research.
- Center for Creative Leadership. (2019). "The Role of Middle Managers: Translators in Organizations." CCL Insights.
- Center for Creative Leadership. (2020). The 70-20-10 Rule for Leadership Development.
- Covey, S. R. (1989). The 7 Habits of Highly Effective People. Simon & Schuster.
- Covey, S. M. R. (2006). The Speed of Trust: The One Thing That Changes Everything. Free Press.
- Drucker, P. (1967). The Effective Executive. Harper & Row.
- Foss, N. J., Pedersen, T., Reinholt, M., & Stea, D. (2015). "Why Middle Managers Are So Important." Harvard Business Review, October 2015.
- Hill, L. A. (2003). Becoming a Manager: How New Managers Master the Challenges of Leadership. Harvard Business Review Press.
- Ibarra, H. (2015). Act Like a Leader, Think Like a Leader. Harvard Business Review Press.
- Ibarra, H., & Scoular, A. (2019). "The Leader as Coach." Harvard Business Review, November–December 2019.
- Katzenbach, J. R., & Smith, D. K. (2005). "The Discipline of Teams." Harvard Business Review, July–August 2005.
- Kouzes, J. M., & Posner, B. Z. (2017). The Leadership Challenge (6th ed.). Wiley.

- McKinsey & Company. (2021). "How Middle Managers Drive Organizational Change." McKinsey Insights.
- Perlow, L. A., Hadley, C. N., & Eun, E. (2017). "Stop the Meeting Madness." Harvard Business Review, July–August 2017.
- Prosci. (2020). Best Practices in Change Management. Prosci Research.
- Watkins, M. (2013). The First 90 Days (Updated ed.). Harvard Business Review Press.
- Zenger, J., & Folkman, J. (2014). The Extraordinary Leader: Turning Good Managers into Great Leaders. McGraw-Hill.
- Zenger, J., & Stinnett, K. (2010). The Extraordinary Coach: How the Best Leaders Help Others Grow. McGraw-Hill.

Emotional Intelligence & Psychological Safety

- American Psychological Association. (2022). Emotional Intelligence in Leadership. Monitor on Psychology, 53(3).
- Barsade, S. G. (2002). "The Ripple Effect: Emotional Contagion and Its Influence on Group Behavior." Administrative Science Quarterly, 47(4), 644–675.
- Edmondson, A. (2018). The Fearless Organization: Creating Psychological Safety in the Workplace for Learning, Innovation, and Growth. Wiley.
- Goleman, D. (1995). Emotional Intelligence: Why It Can Matter More Than IQ. Bantam Books.
- Goleman, D. (1998). Working with Emotional Intelligence. Bantam Books.

- Goleman, D., Boyatzis, R., & McKee, A. (2013). Primal Leadership: Unleashing the Power of Emotional Intelligence. Harvard Business Press.
- Harvard Business Review. (2018). "The Business Case for Emotional Intelligence." Harvard Business Review Digital Articles.
- Harvard Division of Continuing Education. (2021). "How to Improve Your Emotional Intelligence." Professional Development Blog.
- Newman, A., Donohue, R., & Eva, N. (2020). "Psychological Safety, Emotion Regulation, and Empathy as Key Factors in Leadership Effectiveness." Frontiers in Psychology, 11, 1581.
- PMC / National Center for Biotechnology Information. (2023). "Emotional Intelligence: Why It Matters in Change Leadership and Innovation in the 21st Century." Frontiers in Psychology.
- Rozovsky, J. (2015). "The Five Keys to a Successful Google Team." re:Work by Google.

HR, Performance & Accountability

- Chartered Institute of Personnel and Development (CIPD). (2018). Managing Redundancy and Dismissals. CIPD Guide.
- Chartered Institute of Personnel and Development (CIPD). (2021). Performance Management: Everyday Accountability. CIPD Report.
- Gallup. (2015). State of the American Manager: Analytics and Advice for Leaders. Gallup Press.
- Gallup. (2019). It's the Manager: Moving From Boss to Coach. Gallup Press.

- Gallup. (2023). State of the Global Workplace Report. Gallup Press.
- Patterson, K., Grenny, J., Maxfield, D., McMillan, R., & Switzler, A. (2013). Crucial Accountability: Tools for Resolving Violated Expectations, Broken Commitments, and Bad Behavior. McGraw-Hill.
- SHRM. (2015). "The High Cost of a Toxic Employee." SHRM Research.
- SHRM. (2017). "The Real Cost of a Bad Hire." SHRM Research.
- SHRM. (2018). "How to Document and Address Performance Issues." SHRM Toolkit.
- SHRM. (2019). "Handling Employee Terminations with Dignity and Respect." SHRM Resource Center.
- SHRM. (2019). "Performance Management That Makes a Difference." SHRM Research.
- SHRM. (2020). "Effective Performance Improvement Plans (PIPs)." SHRM Toolkit.
- SHRM. (2021). "Termination and Offboarding: HR Best Practices." SHRM Toolkit.

Collaboration & Cross-Department Work

- Cross, R., Rebele, R., & Grant, A. (2016). "Collaborative Overload." Harvard Business Review, January–February 2016.
- Deloitte. (2018). 2018 Global Human Capital Trends: The Rise of the Social Enterprise. Deloitte Insights.
- Deloitte. (2018). The Organization of the Future: Arriving Now. Deloitte Insights.

- Foss, N. J., Pedersen, T., Reinholt, M., & Stea, D. (2015). "Why Middle Managers Are So Important." Harvard Business Review, October 2015.
- Forbes Human Resources Council. (2025, January 3). "20 Best Practices for Strengthening Cross-Departmental Collaboration." Forbes Human Resources Council.
- McKinsey & Company. (2021). "How Middle Managers Drive Organizational Change." McKinsey Insights.
- MIT Sloan Management Review. (2019). "The Value of Constructive Conflict in Teams." MIT Sloan Management Review.

Coaching & Development

- Center for Creative Leadership. (2014). "70-20-10 Model of Learning and Development." CCL Insights.
- CSO Insights. (2019). Fifth Annual Sales Enablement Study. Miller Heiman Group.
- Evered, R., & Selman, J. C. (1989). "Coaching and the Art of Management." Organizational Dynamics, 18(2), 16–32.
- Google People Analytics. (2013). "Project Oxygen: The Eight Behaviors of Great Managers." re:Work by Google.
- Sales Management Association. (2018). Optimizing Sales Coaching Impact. Sales Management Association Research Report.
- Spekit. (2022). The State of Sales Training and Onboarding Report.

Culture, Trust & Engagement

- Center for Creative Leadership. (2020). "Emotional Intelligence and Leadership Effectiveness." CCL Research.
- Covey, S. M. R. (2006). The Speed of Trust: The One Thing That Changes Everything. Free Press.
- Gallup. (2019). It's the Manager: Moving From Boss to Coach. Gallup Press.
- Ofori, W. (2024). "The Silent Message: How Firing Employees Shapes Workplace Culture." LinkedIn Articles.
- Salesforce Research. (2020). State of Sales Report (4th Edition). Salesforce Research.

Learning Agility & Future Skills

- Korn Ferry Institute. (2017). The Self-Disruptive Leader. Korn Ferry Global Research.
- Korn Ferry. (2018). "Learning Agility: Unlock the Power of Potential." Korn Ferry Global Institute.
- Society for Industrial and Organizational Psychology (SIOP). (2010). "Learning Agility as a Predictor of Leadership Success." SIOP White Paper.

Discipline & Performance Principles

- Willink, J., & Babin, L. (2015). Extreme Ownership: How U.S. Navy SEALs Lead and Win. St. Martin's Press.

About the Author

Trevor Weber has spent twenty years building a career in both B2B and B2C sales, working with clients across enterprise, education, government, healthcare, retail, and real estate. His background spans roles as an individual contributor, sales leader, and sales enablement professional, giving him a practical understanding of the challenges sellers face at various stages of their careers.

Trevor is a certified John Maxwell coach and DISC practitioner and holds a Master's degree in Organizational Leadership. Drawing on this blend of hands-on sales experience and leadership training, he equips sellers and managers through both strategy and skill development. His approach blends real-world experience with coaching expertise, making him a trusted resource for sales professionals and leaders alike.

When not working, Trevor enjoys spending time with his wife and four children in Utah. He's happiest outdoors, whether hiking, biking, or exploring new places, and he also pursues his creative side by writing fiction fantasy alongside his professional works on sales and leadership.

Printed in Dunstable, United Kingdom